Contents

Introduction

Language skills underpin just about every aspect of your child's learning and development. From forming relationships with other people, to discovering about the world and how it works, language is the key.

As your child grows older, they will also develop their literacy skills. Literacy is language in its written form. The literate individual is able to read other people's written or printed thoughts, messages and stories and record their own thoughts in writing for others to read. Being literate also means knowing where to find information and how to understand and make sense of what you read – from stories and poems, to newspaper articles, signs, notices and sets of instructions. Learning how to handle a pencil, form letters, produce legible handwriting, spell correctly and express yourself in writing also come under the broad umbrella of literacy.

Given that language and literacy are so important, what should parents and carers be doing to help? If this question unnerves you, the good news is that you don't need any special knowledge or expertise. Simply talking to your child, sharing picture books, playing games and providing easy access to paper, pencils and crayons are far and away the most important things you can do to help your child's language development and provide a foundation for literacy.

This brings us to the purpose of this book. In the coming chapters, we set out to explain the different aspects of language and literacy and look at what you can do to help. It is important to emphasise that this book is not intended to make any parent feel pressurised. Our aim is to look at the value of what you are already doing – and explore ways of developing and making the most of everyday activities such as chatting, reading stories and playing games.

The chapters are as follows:

Chapter 1 Language Development – What to Expect

Chapter 1 looks at why language is so important and traces the developmental milestones for a typical child. It also looks at what you can do if you have any concerns.

Chapter 2 Talking With Your Child

Chapter 2 looks at the importance of conversation and word acquisition. It also suggests practical ways of making the most of conversation, playing word games and helping your child to develop their speech.

Chapter 3 Learning to Listen

Chapter 3 explores why listening skills play such an important part in language development and learning in general. It also suggests practical ways of helping your child develop their listening skills, including some quick and easy games to play.

Chapter 4 Nursery Rhymes

Chapter 4 explains why rhyme is so important to a child's literacy development and suggests games to play with nursery rhymes and rhyming words.

Chapter 5 Sharing Picture Books

Chapter 5 looks at the importance of picture books, how to go about choosing them and ways of making the most of sharing them with your child.

Chapter 6 Exploring Sounds and Letters

Chapter 6 looks at how you can introduce your child to the sounds of language through games such as I Spy – and suggests activities for introducing letters and matching them with their sounds.

Chapter 7 Becoming a Reader

Chapter 7 includes a brief outline of how reading is taught in school and suggests some activities to support and encourage your child as a reader. It also gives tips on hearing your child read once they start to bring home a reading book.

Chapter 8 Becoming a Writer

Chapter 8 explains what the complex process of writing involves. It also looks at ways of encouraging your child to write.

Chapter 9 Helping with Handwriting

Chapter 9 looks specifically at the handwriting element of writing – including how to help your child with their pencil grip and letter formation and what you can do if your child has handwriting difficulties.

Chapter 10 Helping with Spelling

Chapter 10 gives lots of useful tips on how to support your older child's spelling, including spelling rules and tricks and tips for learning spellings.

Early Years Guidance

This section outlines the Early Years guidance and curriculum for England, Scotland, Wales and Northern Ireland.

The book is designed to be dipped into, rather than read from cover to cover. Activities such as talking with your child, helping to develop listening skills, rhyming activities and sharing books are relevant to all age groups. The later chapters are largely aimed at parents whose children have started school, although some children will be reading and writing before Reception or Year 1.

At the end of the book, there is a book list of recommended picture books and a help list of useful websites.

Chapter One

Language Development – What to Expect

The first three years of a child's life are the most important for developing their language skills. During this time, the child passes through what are known as 'critical periods' for acquiring language. Throughout these periods, the child is particularly alert and sensitive to language and it's important that they are exposed to as much speech as possible.

In this chapter, we outline some of the key milestones in a typical child's language development. Although it's useful to know what to expect during the first few years, it's important to remember that these milestones are only averages. Every child develops at their own pace and reaching a milestone later than the norm is usually nothing to worry about.

It can, however, be hard to judge whether or not your child is developing 'normally' and it is common for parents to be anxious – particularly during the early years. If you are concerned about your child's language development, check the 'If you are worried' sections throughout the chapter and see the end of the chapter for advice on seeking professional support.

The first year

During the first 12 months of your baby's life, you will see major developments in their language skills.

Before birth

It is now known that babies can hear before they are born, possibly as early as 24 weeks gestation. If you want to talk, sing or play music to your unborn child, there is every reason to suppose that they will hear these sounds – even if they cannot yet make sense of them.

The newborn

From birth, babies show signs of preferring the human voice to any other noises, and during the first 12 weeks they start turning towards you when you speak. Talking, singing, cooing and making eye contact with your baby is an important means of helping them learn the communication process (for more on this, see chapter 2). Babies also respond more positively to soft, gentle voice tones than sharp, loud noises – useful to remember when you want to calm your baby or hold their attention.

The first six months

Between four and six months, your baby will start responding to more subtle changes in the tone of your voice – again, useful to know when you want to soothe your baby or excite their interest. They also become much more interested in the different noises within their environment – the sound of a ringing telephone, the beep of a car horn, the mew of a cat or a music CD. Involving your baby in everyday life will give them the opportunity to absorb human speech and the sounds of the world around them. This is also a good time to introduce simple toys that make sounds when the baby plays with them.

As every parent soon discovers, babies are very well able to communicate through sound. During the first four months, your baby will cry, gurgle and coo and it becomes increasingly easy to tell whether they are communicating hunger, pain, loneliness or contentment.

From four to five months, the 'babbling' stage of language acquisition takes off. Babbling enables the baby to experiment with speech-like noises and increasingly the babbling takes on the natural cadences of proper speech.

Babbling can consist of a single repeated syllable such as 'da-da-da-da' or a mix of syllables such as 'ma-ma-bu-do-ba-ba'. It is no coincidence that the baby name for mother is 'ma-ma' (or similar) in so many languages.

The next six months

Between six and 12 months, babies start responding to their own names by turning and looking at the speaker. They also become able to recognise familiar people and items by name – so, for example, if you ask your child 'where's teddy?' they will be able to look at or reach for teddy.

During this stage in your baby's development their babbling becomes more complex, with a wider range of consonants (b, c, d, g and so on) and both long and short vowel sounds (such as the long 'ay' sound in 'hay' and the short 'a' sound in 'hat').

It is also fun to introduce interactive finger plays at around this time, as your baby will now be able to participate fully and enjoy the movements, sounds and rhythms of the rhyme (see chapter 4 for more on this).

The first word

At around 12 months, babies produce their first word – typically, a common but significant word such as 'mama', 'dada', 'cat' or 'ball'. This means that the child has gained enough control over their lips, tongue and vocal chords to intentionally articulate a word. It also shows their understanding that a single word can be attached to an object or person – an important stage in their conceptual development. A child's first word is therefore quite different from babbling, even though it may sound similar.

If your child's first word has not appeared by 18 months, try increasing the one-to-one time you spend with the child. Set yourself a target of at least 30 minutes a day (not necessarily all in one go) and focus exclusively on the child – talking, sharing picture books, playing and generally interacting with them. Encourage other family members to do the same.

'At around 12 months, babies produce their first word – typically, a common but significant word such as "mama", or "dada".'

The second year

'It's common for children to make a "language leap" leading up to their second birthday.'

During your child's second year, they will develop the ability to point to a named and recognisable person, object, body part or picture in a book. They also become able to follow simple instructions – although it's a good idea to help them understand the instruction by following it through with them, or prompting them with actions and gestures. From around 18 months, they should be able to follow simple instructions without an accompanying gesture – in other words, by understanding the words alone.

During this period, your child's collection of words will grow rapidly. It's common for children to make a 'language leap' leading up to their second birthday and by two years the child will have between 150 and 300 words (although there's no need to be concerned if your child has fewer words at this stage). The pronunciation of words becomes clearer and the child also starts putting together two words to ask a question or label an object or person – for example, 'where nana?' or 'doggy woof'. Repeating a word or a phrase over and over again (known as 'echolalia') is common in this age group.

If you are worried

It may be worth seeking advice if your one to two-year-old child:

- Speaks very little or not at all.
- Does not seem to hear what you say or be able to listen.
- Appears to have difficulty understanding you.

It is, however, important to remember that children develop at very different rates, particularly with the number of words they can say by age two.

The 'Seeking further advice' section on page 15 has more about who to contact if you are worried.

The third year

Your child's vocabulary will explode during their third year, reaching anything from 300 to 1,000 words by the time they turn three. They will also start using the pronouns 'I', 'me' and 'you', a small number of prepositions such as 'in', 'on' and 'under' and some simple plurals such as 'cats' and 'toys'.

Between the ages of two and three, your child will become able to follow an instruction with two parts – for example, 'find your ball and put it in the toy box'. They also start to construct their own three or even four-word sentences ('doggy in nana car'). This is a sign that they understand how to structure language and use it to communicate. Most of what a child says should now be intelligible to their nearest and dearest.

Three-year-olds often become frustrated when they are not able to make themselves understood. By now, they realise that talking is a means of expressing their thoughts and needs to others – but the language tools they possess haven't yet caught up with the complexity of their ideas. Whenever possible, it's well worth taking the time to tease out what your child is trying to tell you. Being understood is an important part of becoming a happy and confident communicator.

'It's well worth taking the time to tease out what your child is trying to tell you. Being understood is an important part of becoming a happy and confident communicator.'

The fourth year

During their fourth year, your child will become able to understand the simple but very important question words 'what?', 'who?' and 'where?' This means that they can understand most simple questions about their familiar environment and daily experiences, for example: 'what jumper do you want to wear?' or 'who is coming to play today?' They should also be able to say their name and their age when asked.

Vocabulary acquisition continues growing apace and by the time they turn four, many children will know the names of most common everyday objects, body parts and animals. They will also be able to recognise and name a few colours and repeat numbers (one, two, three).

Children of this age love to talk about their life experiences at nursery, playing with friends, visiting the park or going on a special outing. You can expect your four-year-old to use sentences of four to five words and their grammar (the arrangement of words in a sentence) will be largely correct by the end of the fourth year. At this stage, 'outsiders' should be able to understand most of what the child says.

The fifth year

During their fifth year, the child's ability to answer questions about a story takes off – as does their ability to make up their own stories. The child will also tend to talk to him or herself during activities and use language in their make-believe games. In other words, language becomes a significant part of the four to five-year-old's play.

The child's spontaneous use of describing words for objects and actions also develops swiftly during this period. This enables them to communicate that 'the hedgehog is prickly' or 'the horsey runs fast'. They can also understand comparative adjectives to describe contrasting qualities – 'the blue pencil is longer than the red one' or 'the mummy elephant is bigger than the baby elephant'.

The child's speech is generally fully intelligible by now, even though they may still have difficulties articulating certain words or sounds; for example, a lisp or problems pronouncing 'r' and 'th' are common at around this time. Sentences will become much more complex and lengthy – 'Nana gave Freddy his dinner and Freddy barked and barked cos he was happy and he gobbled all his dinner up and spilled some on the floor'. The child will also be able to tell a lengthy story on a given topic, particularly if they have had lots of stories read to them and absorbed story structure and language (see chapter 5 for more on this).

If you are worried

It may be worth seeking advice if your three to five-year-old child:

- Struggles to produce a number of sounds (mispronunciation of a few sounds is common).

- Starts to stutter – a speech difficulty that often emerges between three and four years.

- Does not appear to be learning new words.

- Struggles to join words together to make a sentence.

- Is difficult for people outside close family members to understand – particularly from four onwards.

- Finds it hard to listen to instructions or forgets them as soon as they are said.

- Shows other signs of hearing difficulties, as they often emerge between three and four years.

'Remember that every child is different. It's not uncommon for a child to be speaking very little at two but catch up by the time they are three.'

Seeking further advice

If you find yourself worrying about your child's language development, don't forget that every child is different. Making slower than average progress is often nothing to be concerned about and it's not uncommon for a child to be speaking very little at two but catch up by the time they are three. Children growing up in a bilingual family or younger siblings in a large family of children, may also have slower speech development. This usually sorts itself out as the child gets older.

At the same time, it's important not to ignore your worries for too long. If there is a problem, there's a lot that can be done to help and the sooner a child is given support, the better. Your health visitor or GP will be able to make an initial assessment and refer your child to a speech and language therapist if necessary. They will also be able to check your child's hearing, as this can be the cause of delayed speech development. If your child is at nursery or has started school, another option is to get advice from the school's special needs co-ordinator (SENCO).

Summing Up

During their first six months, your baby will:

- Show a preference for the human voice over other sounds.
- Turn towards you when you speak.
- Communicate through cries, gurgles and cooing.
- Start to babble.

During their second six months, your baby will:

- Start responding to their name.
- Be able to look at and reach for a familiar person or object when named.
- Develop more complex babbling.

During their second year, your child will:

- Produce their first word (usually between 12 and 18 months).
- Be able to point to a familiar person or object when named.
- Follow simple instructions accompanied by gestures up to around 18 months and without gestures from 18 months onwards.
- Have approximately 150 to 300 words by the age of two.
- Put two words together to ask a question or label an object.

During their third year, your child will:

- Probably experience a 'language explosion' around the start of this year.
- Have between 300 and 1000 words by their third birthday.
- Start using pronouns, simple prepositions and plurals.

- Follow two-part instructions ('find the ball and put it in the toy box').
- Combine three or four words to make sentences.
- Be mostly intelligible to family members.

During the fourth year, your child will:

- Know the names of most common objects, animals, body parts and colours by their fourth birthday.
- Understand the question words 'who?', 'where?' and 'when?' and be able to answer simple questions based on familiar events.
- Love to talk about their everyday experiences.
- Be mostly intelligible to people outside immediate family.

During their fifth year, your child will:

- Make up their own stories and use language in make-believe play.
- Spontaneously use words to describe actions and objects ('run fast', 'prickly hedgehog').
- Be able to construct long and complex sentences when speaking.
- Be fully intelligible, even if they have a lisp or difficulties pronouncing certain sounds.

If you are worried:

- Remember that children develop at different rates and language milestones are only averages.
- Ask for advice from your GP, health visitor or the SENCO at your child's nursery or school.

Chapter Two

Talking With Your Child

Talking with your child is essential to their developing language skills. In this chapter, we look at the importance of conversation and how to make the most of talking with your child. We also look at how young children build their vocabulary and offer some tips and suggestions for learning new words.

The importance of conversation

Talking with your child is one of the single most important things you can do to help their language and literacy development. There are many reasons why conversation is so important.

Absorbing new words and speech patterns

Conversation exposes the child to new words and patterns of speech (how words are ordered so that they make sense). It also encourages them to try out spoken language for themselves.

Bonding with your child

Conversation is a great way to strengthen your bonds with your child. It also gives you an insight into their thoughts and feelings.

Forming relationships

Conversation is central to relationships with other people. Conversing with you will help your child learn how to take turns in a conversation, listen to their conversational partner and respond appropriately.

'Talking with your child is one of the single most important things you can do to help their language and literacy development.'

Learning about the world

Children learn a huge amount from conversation. Even simple, everyday conversational topics give children lots of information about the world and how it works.

Conversing with your child

You are the best person to converse with your child. Studies show that conversations between parent and child are much richer and more complex than conversations between teacher and child. Because you know your child, you are better at understanding what they are saying – which is good for their self-confidence and growing identity as a communicator.

Programmed for language

As we saw in chapter 1, the young child passes through a critical period for language development. During this time, the child's brain is wired to absorb language – including more than one language in a bilingual family. They will never again be able to pick up language so easily or effectively.

Interacting with your baby

So what can you do to make the most of this vital time in your child's life? Interacting with your baby is vital. Making eye contact and responding to a baby's smiles, gurgles and babbling helps the baby learn how to communicate with other people.

Babies also learn how to interact through watching and listening to adults and older children. Gradually, they absorb the subtle conventions of conversation such as taking turns at speaking, listening to the other person and responding to what they have said. However, this can only happen when the child is with other people. Never underestimate how much a child absorbs from simply being in the midst of family and friends.

'Modelling' language

Whenever you talk with your young child, you are modelling spoken language and the process of conversation. In other words, you are showing your child how to speak. As you converse with your child, listen out for what they are trying to communicate, based on your knowledge of their interests and recent experiences. Help them by interpreting their words, repeating their words back to them and giving them prompts.

As already mentioned, this is where parents are so important as conversational partners. Because you know your child better than anyone else, you have a huge head start in making sense of what your child is saying – which in turn, enables you to develop the child's words into a rich, extensive and meaningful conversation.

Modelling language

Three-year-old Gemma loved helping to feed her grandma's cat, Jacey. When Gemma informed her mother that 'Gacey go mow mow.' Mum knew exactly what her daughter was talking about because she knew all about her interest in Jacey. This 'inside information' enabled Gemma's mother to respond in a way that modelled the correct pronunciation of 'Jacey' and developed Gemma's statement into a conversation – 'Yes, Gemma, Jacey goes "meow". Did she go "meow" when she had her dinner?'

Conversational opportunities

As your child's speech develops, their involvement in conversation will become more extensive. The best way of helping your child with their language skills is simply to converse with them as often as possible. Don't feel that you have to set aside 'quality time' for conversation. Just chat whenever you get the chance – on the way to nursery or school, while making dinner and before bed. Go with the flow of the conversation and don't worry about picking 'educational' topics. Talking through the practicalities of cleaning teeth or getting dressed is just as valuable as discussing why the sky is blue.

'Chat with your child whenever you get the chance – on the way to nursery or school, while making dinner and before bed.'

Responding to questions

One simple way to increase conversation with your child is to respond to as many of their questions as possible. A question is a priceless opportunity to engage with your child and help them to develop both their thinking and their language skills. Children are inexperienced in the ways of the world, and they need to test out their world view on a 'more experienced other' – ideally, you.

And if you don't know the answer to a question, don't worry. Not many of us can explain why the sky is blue – but that needn't prevent us from discussing the possibilities! The Russian psychologist Vygotsky suggested that you can explain just about anything to a young child – as long as you pitch it at the right level. Give it a go. Young children are natural philosophers and you may find yourself looking at things in a whole new light, once you enter their world through conversation.

'A question is a priceless opportunity to engage with your child and help them to develop both their thinking and their language skills.'

Words, words, words

Young children are programmed to pick up words. As a parent, you do not have to be self-conscious about teaching your child new words. At the same time, there are some quick, easy and fun ways of maximising your child's vocabulary acquisition, without pressurising either you or the child.

New words in context

Most parents are good at adjusting their speech to their child's level of understanding. However, don't feel too restricted in the vocabulary you use. As long as you use words in context, your child will understand your meaning. Young children are also much more likely to remember new words when they come across them naturally, as a part of everyday activities such as cooking or swimming. For example, when you bake with your child, talk about the different actions and utensils – 'Can you stir the mixture with the whisk?' It doesn't matter if the words 'mixture' or 'whisk' are unfamiliar to the child; they will soon pick up your meaning because you are using those words in context.

Word pronunciation

In their attempts to grapple with a new word, young children tend to come up with some delightful mispronunciations. Although these words often earn a special place in a family's lexicon, many children become quite cross if their mispronunciation is repeated back to them with amusement. Help your child in a positive way by responding with the correct pronunciation. For example:

Child: 'Weex comin to pay.'

Parent: 'Yes, sweetheart, Felix is coming to play after lunch.'

Conversing with your child – a checklist

▪ Make eye contact and respond to your baby's gurgles and babbling.

▪ Keep your baby with you in social situations so they can absorb spoken language.

▪ Model spoken language by repeating your child's words back to them, using correct pronunciation and a fuller sentence.

▪ Don't worry about setting aside 'quality time' for conversation. Just chat freely with your child whenever you have the chance.

▪ Follow up questions as extensively as possible – and if you don't know the answer, have fun discussing the possibilities!

▪ Don't be afraid to use unfamiliar words – context will help the child understand your meaning.

'Young children are more likely to remember new words when they come across them naturally, as a part of everyday activities such as cooking or swimming.'

Learning new words with books and games

Picture books, word books, board games and card games are a great way of introducing new vocabulary.

Picture books

The context of the story and pictures in a picture book helps the child to understand the meaning of new words. For example, in Pat Hutchins's picture book *Rosie's Walk*, published by Random House, the words tell you that Rosie the hen 'walks under the beehives'. It is quite possible that the words 'under' and 'beehives' are unfamiliar to your child, but it doesn't matter because the picture shows so clearly what 'walking under the beehives' actually means.

Picture books are also great for triggering interesting conversations with your child. See chapter 5 for more on this.

Word books

Word books are specifically designed to introduce young children to new words. Look out for books that label detailed scenes such as 'at the supermarket'. This enables the child to see the names of objects within context and recognise the conceptual link between separate objects (for example, 'trousers', 'shirt', 'dress', 'jumper' and 'coat' go together because they are all clothes). Looking at the picture of an object alongside its written name is also helpful for children who are starting to read.

See the book list for some recommended word books and picture dictionaries.

Board games and card games

Look out for games that focus on words. Picture lotto, picture dominoes, snap and tray puzzles are fun to play with and they also help children to learn new words, as well as giving you the opportunity to interact with your child.

Word activities and different kinds of words

Although young children pick up words naturally, you can help them to develop a wide-ranging vocabulary by introducing different types of words.

Naming words

The grammatical term for naming words is 'nouns'. Nouns are the first words that babies pick up. As soon as your child is able to name some items, try a simple naming game such as 'I went shopping and I bought . . . ' In order to play the game, wander round the house with your child, choosing and naming objects to put in your shopping basket.

With older children (three-plus) find groups of objects such as fruit, toys or items of clothing. This helps the child to see the connection between separate objects.

Action words

The grammatical term for action words is 'verbs'. Verbs are easy to introduce into everyday conversation. When walking to the shops, challenge your children to run to the lamp post and back before you count to ten; when out in the garden, give them an obstacle course – can they crawl around the bush and wriggle through the play tunnel?

This is a useful game for children with lots of energy to burn off and also a quick and easy way of encouraging your child to be active.

Action describing words

The grammatical term for words that describe an action is 'adverbs'. Adverbs make our communications more interesting and accurate. With older children, challenge them to jump slowly and jump quickly, whisper quietly or shout loudly, pat the dog gently and tap firmly on their drum.

Size words

'Size words' help us to explain ourselves more accurately. When your child is drawing, ask them to draw a huge giant and a tiny mouse or a fat dinosaur and a thin snake. During a boring car journey, challenge them to look out for a gigantic lorry, a tall tree, a long hedge, a little car, a big sign and so on.

Colour words

Colour words can be introduced during art activities and as a part of everyday life. With little ones, look out for opportunities to name the basic colours (blue, red, yellow, green, orange, purple, brown, black, white). For example, do they want to wear the orange T-shirt or the green T-shirt today? With older ones, try introducing names for different shades such as crimson, emerald and tangerine.

Texture words

Texture words such as 'prickly', 'soft' and 'crunchy' describe how an object feels. The 'feely game' (for the three-plus age group) is great fun and helps the child develop their vocabulary. Choose some items with different textures and shapes, for example; a feather, a sponge, a pine cone, a hairbrush, a book, a spoon and a teddy bear. Fill a bag with the items, feel an item, name it and then have a go at describing its texture.

'Encourage your child to talk about their feelings and use different words to describe their emotions and physical state.'

'Feelings' words

'Feelings' words such as 'happy', 'sad', 'bored', 'hot' and 'tired' are important in helping us to communicate how we feel. Encourage your child to talk about their feelings and use different words to describe their emotions and physical state. You can also talk about the feelings of characters in TV programmes and picture books.

Give older children a sentence to finish: 'Going to the park makes me feel happy/excited/cheerful' 'Arguing with my friend makes me feel angry/upset/sad'. If the child is receptive, talk about the event and why it makes them feel a particular way.

Position words

The grammatical term for words that describe position is 'prepositions'. Prepositions include words such as 'up', 'on' and 'behind'. They are important words for your child to learn as they help them to give and follow instructions.

Offer your child little challenges to set the words in context: 'Can you hide *behind* the sofa?' 'Can you run *around* the swings?' 'Can you jump *over* the puddle?'

This is another game that is useful for children with lots of energy to burn off – and something you can do on the spur of the moment.

Summing Up

- Communicating with babies and enabling them to absorb spoken language is important for language development.

- You, the parent, are the most important conversational partner for your child as you are best placed to understand their communications.

- It is important to chat to your child and respond to as many of their questions as possible.

- Introducing new and unfamiliar words in context will help your child understand their meaning.

- Picture books, word books, card and board games are great ways to introduce new words to children.

- Words fall into different categories, for example: naming words, action words and position words. Try the games in the last section of this chapter to introduce different types of words to your child.

Chapter Three
Learning to Listen

Listening is an essential part of communicating with others and the ability to listen effectively is also central to learning. Listening is a skill and there are many ways of helping your child to develop good listening habits. In this chapter, we look at the importance of listening and suggest some simple techniques and games to help your child develop their listening skills.

About listening

When thinking about how to help a child's listening skills, it's useful to draw a distinction between 'listening' and 'hearing'. Although we hear sounds all around us, such as the roar of the traffic outside or the whirr of a washing machine, we don't tend to register these sounds. In contrast, listening is an active process. Listening means taking on board what we hear and listening to someone talk involves processing their words and responding to what has been said.

Becoming an active listener is a skill that children can learn. If your older child has developed the habit of 'switching off', it's also perfectly possible to help them improve their listening skills and learn how to engage in a conversation.

Listening to instructions

Instructions make up a good proportion of our interaction with each other and the ability to follow instructions plays an important part in helping your child to function in nursery, school and other social situations.

Encouraging your child to listen to your instructions has several benefits. Perhaps most importantly, instructions such as 'hold my hand when we cross the road' will help keep your child safe. Instructions are also essential for activities

'Listening is an active process. Listening means taking on board what we hear – and listening to someone talk involves processing their words and responding to what has been said.'

such as playing a board game or learning how to swim. Much of your child's school life will revolve around listening to and following instructions – from grasping what standards of behaviour are expected to learning how to add up.

The following suggestions are simple, straightforward and easy to slip into everyday life.

A physical link

When you want your child to listen to you, squat or kneel at their level and make eye contact. It's also useful to hold their hand or gently position them in front of you by holding their elbows. Making a physical link helps to set the scene for making a verbal link.

Keep it short

'Help your young child to understand an instruction by acting it out with them.'

We all tend to switch off when we have to listen to unnecessary detail. Keep your instructions short, simple and to the point.

Act it out

Help your young child to understand an instruction by acting it out with them. For example, ask your little one to 'give the teddy to Nana' and then help them pass the teddy to Nana.

Be age appropriate

Children are much more likely to listen to instructions if they are tailored to the age and understanding of the child.

- Between six months and a year, many children can respond to a simple instruction such as 'give the ball to Grandpa' - as long as Grandpa is smiling at them with outstretched hands.

- From 12 months to two years, many children can follow a simple, one-part instruction such as 'throw the ball', without any prompting.

- From two to three years, many children are able to understand and follow two-part instructions such as 'find the ball and put it in the toy box'.

- From three to four years, many children are able to understand the question words 'who?', 'where?' and 'what?' By this age they will not be so reliant on concrete objects, enabling you to talk about items that are not present, for example: 'Where did you put Grandpa's ball?'

- From four years onwards, children can understand most of what is said to them and you can develop and expand on the instructions you give them.

It's important to remember that this is just a rough guide and that children develop at very different rates. Don't worry too much if your child does not seem able to do certain things at a set age. Similarly, don't feel restricted by this guidance. If you think your child can understand and respond to more complicated instructions, give it a go.

If you are worried

If you are worried about your child's hearing, see chapter 1.

'If a child is bombarded with instructions and negative statements, they learn to switch off.'

Repeating back

If you suspect your older child is not really listening to you, ask them to repeat back what you have just said. It is, however, important to keep your tone of voice as light-hearted as possible. Even if you are frustrated, try to avoid making the child feel as though you are testing them.

Don't overdo it

Try to avoid giving too many instructions and orders – particularly if they are mostly of the 'don't do that' kind. If a child is bombarded with instructions and negative statements, they learn to switch off.

When to intervene – a checklist

When trying to decide whether to intervene with a negative or controlling instruction, ask yourself:

- Is my child doing something unsafe?
- Is my child hurting or disturbing another person?
- Is my child damaging something?
- Is my child behaving inappropriately?

If the answer to all these questions is 'no', do you really need to intervene? Saving your instructions for things that really matter means that your child is much more likely to listen to what you say.

Following through

Encourage your child to follow through an instruction or request. This is particularly important with practical, day-to-day instructions, such as asking your child to stop playing with the baskets in a supermarket queue. When you are harassed or distracted, it's easy to give an instruction and then let it go when your child ignores you. It will, however, pay off in the long run if you can be consistent about following things through.

Listening to stories

Listening to stories is a great way of helping your child to develop active listening skills. A good story engages their interest so that listening becomes automatic. Although we will focus on stories and picture books in chapter 5, the following tips look at how stories can be used as an aid to developing good listening habits.

- Pick stories to suit your child's interests. The more interested they are, the more attentively they will listen.

- If your child is a 'wriggler', try to avoid pressurising them to sit quietly, as this will turn story time into a negative experience.

- Once you have finished, talk to your child about the story. You may be surprised at how much they have absorbed, even if they didn't appear to be listening at the time.

- Don't persevere with a story if your child has lost interest. Go back to it later or find a different book. If you can keep story time a positive experience, your child will be more likely to listen attentively.

- Try the shared story-telling technique. Start off with a sentence, then let the child tell the next part of the story and continue taking turns until the story is completed. Children love making up stories and the turn-taking process encourages them to listen.

- Look out for story CDs so that your child can listen to stories independently.

Being a good role model

You are your child's first and most important teacher and being a good listener yourself plays an important part in helping your child develop their listening skills. Check out the following list and aim to introduce any listening habits that you are not already practising.

Attentive body language

Eye contact is not just a way of checking that your child is attending to you. It also shows the child that you are attending to them. Positive body language is an important part of listening to someone and helps you to be a good role model for your child.

'Being a good listener yourself plays an important part in helping your child develop their listening skills.'

Ignore distractions

When your child is speaking, try to show them that they are your priority. If at all possible, ignore interruptions such as the telephone. If you do need to break off, explain that you will continue listening just as soon as you have dealt with the distraction and do your best to keep your promise. If your child knows that you will listen to them, they are much more likely to listen to you.

Be honest

'Give your child time to complete what they are saying – and avoid interrupting them, cutting them off or taking over what they are trying to say.'

Being the perfect listener is not always practical. If you simply don't have time to listen to your child, be honest with them and promise that you will listen to them later. There's nothing more demoralising than trying to talk to someone who is clearly not listening – and your child will probably see through any attempts at pretence on your part, particularly if you are busy doing something else.

Be patient

Even if you are not particularly interested in what your child is saying, it's important to listen carefully and respond positively. It's also important to listen in a relaxed manner when your child is struggling to express themselves. Give them time to complete what they are saying and avoid interrupting them, cutting them off or taking over what they are trying to say.

Be interesting

Make the most of any questions and conversational topics that your child brings up. If you talk together about things that interest them, they are more likely to listen to what you have to say. Watch out also for signs that your child is losing interest in the conversation – and don't expect them to carry on listening beyond their natural attention span.

Turn off the TV

While there is nothing wrong with TV and other screen time activities in moderation, excess exposure does not help a child to develop their listening skills. Screen information can be hard for a child to register and digest – so it's important to give them plenty of 'real life' interaction.

Encouraging your child to listen – a checklist

▪ Keep your baby with you in social situations so they can listen to and absorb spoken language.

▪ Follow up your child's questions and comments with conversation. If you respond to their interests, they will find it easier to listen to what you are saying.

▪ Wherever possible, drop down to the child's level. Make eye contact and gently hold their hand or arm.

▪ When you want your child to listen, try to avoid distracting background noise. Switch off the TV, radio or CD player.

▪ Be a role model and listen carefully to your child whenever you can. This will help them learn how to be a good listener.

▪ Use stories to help your child develop the listening habit.

Listening games

Try these games to encourage your child to develop their listening skills. Each game is quick and simple and most of them can be played on the spur of the moment.

Run to the bush

When you are out on a walk, challenge your children to run to a given destination – 'Run to the blue gate and back before I count to ten.' In order to meet the challenge, the child has to listen to and remember the instruction.

Adjust the challenge to suit the age of the child. Younger ones can simply run to the nearest tree and back, whereas older ones can run to the blue gate, on to the blossom tree and then touch the lamp post on their way back. This is a good game for children with lots of energy to burn off and also useful if you want to increase your child's exercise.

Guess the sound

Gather a collection of objects such as a bunch of keys, a newspaper, a baby's rattle, a whistle, a zip and a guitar. Ask your child to close their eyes and listen carefully while you make a sound with one of the items. Can they guess what is making the sound? Let younger ones see the items before you play the game.

Animal characters

Make up a story with lots of familiar animal characters, such as a sheep, a cat, a dog, a chicken, a pig and a cow. Ask your child to listen out for each character and make an appropriate noise (baa, meow, woof woof) whenever an animal is mentioned. This is a useful game for passing time on a car or train journey.

Silly statements

Come up with some silly statements. Ask your child to listen carefully to a statement and then tell you why it's silly. For example: 'It's hot today so I'm going to wear my scarf and gloves when I walk the dog.' You can also have fun making silly statements when your child isn't expecting them – 'We're going to see Granny now – put your toy cars back in the fridge and find your shoes.'

Odd one out

Give the child a string of words and ask them to tell you the odd one out. For example, 'dog', 'cat', 'house', 'pig'. Give older children longer lists with more subtle differences, such as 'apple', 'pear', 'potato', 'grape', 'orange', 'banana'.

Can you draw?

For this game, you need clipboards, paper and coloured crayons. Sit back-to-back with your child and take it in turns to give each other instructions, for example: 'Draw a tree with yellow leaves.' Make the instructions more complex for older children – 'Draw a stripy ginger cat with a blue bow and a curly tail.' How carefully did they listen to your instructions and could they remember them?

Story illustrations

Ask your child to draw a picture illustrating an event or character from a story. How much do they remember about the event or character and how much have they managed to include?

Silly Simon

Stand in front of the child and give them instructions – either, 'Silly Simon says clap your hands' or just 'clap your hands.' Ask your child to listen carefully and only follow the instruction if it begins with 'Silly Simon says'. For older ones, have fun with the 'silly' theme – 'Silly Simon says put the toothpaste in the fridge' or 'walk across the ceiling.'

Summing Up

■ Listening skills are central to learning and to communicating with others.

■ There is a difference between 'hearing' and 'listening'. Listening is an active process that involves registering and making sense of what you hear.

■ Encourage your child to listen to instructions. This will help them throughout their schooldays and beyond.

■ Listening to stories is an important way of helping your child develop their listening skills.

■ Help your child to develop the listening habit by being a good listener yourself.

■ Help your child develop their listening skills by playing lots of listening games.

Chapter Four

Nursery Rhymes

Nursery rhymes have been around for centuries. Every culture has their own traditional rhymes and they make up an important part of childhood. In this chapter, we look at why nursery rhymes are so important and how you can make the most of them. At the end of the chapter, there is also a section with some rhyming games to play with your child.

Why are nursery rhymes important?

Nursery rhymes help your child's language and literacy development in lots of different ways.

- Many nursery rhymes contain alliteration. This is where some or all of the words in a phrase or sentence begin with the same sound, for example; 'Jack and Jill' or 'sing a song of sixpence'. Alliterative phrases help the child pick up on a particular sound and become more alert to the sounds of language.

- The rhythms of a nursery rhyme help the child absorb the patterns and structures of spoken language.

- The rhythm of a nursery rhyme breaks the word into its separate syllables, e.g. 'Hump-ty Dump-ty'. This is useful for children when they start to read and write.

- Rhyming words enable children to discover that some words sound similar, e.g. Jill/hill, muffet/tuffet, rye/pie. This lays foundations for spelling as well as reading, because words that rhyme often have a similar spelling.

- Rhythm and rhyme are appealing to the ear, which makes nursery rhymes fun to recite. The rhythms and rhyming words attract the child's attention and make the nursery rhyme easier to remember.

- Many children's authors borrow characters from nursery rhymes (Janet and

'Rhythm and rhyme are appealing to the ear – which makes nursery rhymes fun to recite and easy to remember.'

Allan Ahlberg's *Each Peach Pear Plum* is a classic example). If your child knows their nursery rhymes, they will love coming across these familiar characters in a new setting.

- Familiarity with nursery rhymes gives your child a connection with everyone else who knows the same rhyme – from their friends at playgroup to children's TV presenters!

- Playgroups, nurseries and reception teachers often use nursery rhymes as a link between home and school. Your child's nursery or reception teacher may ask if your child knows any rhymes from home so that they can use the same ones in school. They may also give you a list of rhymes to share with your child at home.

Nursery rhymes and our heritage

Nursery rhymes are a part of our cultural heritage. Over the centuries, they have been handed down from parent to child and many rhymes have their roots in historical events. For example, 'Mary Mary Quite Contrary' is said to refer to Queen Mary I, while 'The Grand Old Duke of York' dates back to the Wars of the Roses.

The history of nursery rhymes

If you are interested in the history of nursery rhymes, Peter and Iona Opie's *Oxford Dictionary of Nursery Rhymes* includes historical notes and lots of traditional illustrations. Some older children also enjoy uncovering the history of the rhymes they knew and loved as little ones.

Nursery rhymes and your family roots

For children growing up in the UK, there are lots of old favourites which crop up time and time again in stories, TV programmes and at school. However, your child's experience of nursery rhymes should include rhymes from your family's cultural background. If you have roots outside the UK, sing and recite rhymes to reflect your cultural traditions and pass them on to your child's teacher so they can share them with the whole group.

Making the most of nursery rhymes

Simply sharing lots of nursery rhymes is the most important thing, but you can also make the most of a nursery rhyme with the following ideas.

When to begin

Start singing nursery rhymes to your baby from birth and before if you want to. With very young babies, choose soft, gentle rhymes such as 'Rock-a-bye-Baby' and 'Bye Baby Bunting'. Increase the number of rhymes you sing as the baby grows older, and introduce some more energetic rhymes such as 'Humpty Dumpty' and 'The Grand Old Duke of York'.

Finger plays

Finger plays are rhymes with hand movements. They are great for engaging the child because they offer movement as well as rhythm and rhyme. They also introduce children to the idea of interpreting words through movement – a good foundation for drama and dance.

Finger plays introduce many different types of movement. In just one well-known finger play, 'Incey Wincey Spider', the movements range from the simple (wiggling fingers to represent rain coming down) to the complex (matching alternate thumbs to little fingers to represent the spider climbing up the spout).

If you want to expand your collection of finger plays and nursery rhymes with hand movements, see the book list for some recommended nursery rhyme collections. An Internet search for 'finger plays' will also produce lots of suggestions.

Add actions and sound effects

Young children love nursery rhymes with actions and sound effects. Try being Humpty Dumpty falling off the wall, or the Grand Old Duke of York marching up to the top of the hill. What noises did the cow make when it jumped over the moon, or Little Bo Peep's sheep, or the pig that Tom the piper's son stole?

Anywhere and everywhere

Nursery rhymes can be sung or recited just about anywhere and on the spur of the moment. A nursery rhyme with actions is a positive way of distracting a child who is misbehaving. Along with finger plays, they also make a simple way of keeping your child entertained while waiting at the bus stop or for a doctor's appointment.

Clap the rhythm

When you sing or recite a nursery rhyme, clap along with your child. This helps the child tune into the rhythm of the nursery rhyme.

Make a story

'A nursery rhyme with actions is a positive way of distracting a child who is misbehaving.'

With older children, you can develop the nursery rhyme into a more complex story. What did little Miss Muffet say when the spider appeared? What did the little boy who lived down the lane do with Baa Baa Black Sheep's wool? Where did the dish and the spoon run away to and what did they do when they got there?

Enjoy the rhyming words

Once your child knows a nursery rhyme well, let them finish off each line by themselves – 'Jack and . . . /Went up the . . . ' This will encourage them to focus on the rhyming word at the end of each sentence.

Create your own version

Older children love to make up their own rhymes and they can be surprisingly inventive. Nonsense versions such as 'Jack and Jill/Went up the Bill' will cause great amusement. Once they understand what makes a rhyming word, children also love coming up with funny non-rhyming words – 'Jack and Jill/Went up the potato'.

Nursery rhyme snacks

Food crops up in nursery rhymes time and time again – and it makes a good excuse for singing or reciting a particular rhyme. Try the following:

- When you have a boiled egg for breakfast, draw Humpty's face on the shell with felt pen and recite the rhyme.

- If you have hot cross buns as an Easter snack, sing the 'Hot Cross Buns' rhyme. Older children love punning with this particular rhyme – 'hot cross mummies'!

- When you have a pie for pudding, sing 'Sing a Song of Sixpence' and check carefully for blackbirds when you cut into it!

- Sing 'Half a Pound of Tu'penny Rice' when you have a rice dish for dinner, 'Polly Put the Kettle On' when you make a cup of tea and 'Pat-a-cake, pat-a-cake, Baker's Man' when you do some baking.

Can you and your child come up with any more food nursery rhymes?

Making the most of nursery rhymes – a checklist

- Introduce nursery rhymes from birth.
- Sing nursery rhymes anywhere and everywhere.
- Add hand movements, actions and sound effects.
- Clap to the rhythms.
- Link rhymes with food and other daily activities.
- Encourage your older child to:
  Finish off the rhyming words.
  Make up their own nonsense rhymes.
  Develop a favourite rhyme into a story.

Nursery rhyme books, posters and CDs

Nursery rhymes are part of an oral tradition. They have been recited by parents and grandparents over the centuries and until the last 100 years or so, many of the adults who passed them on to their children would not have been able to read or write.

Today, we are lucky enough to have nursery rhyme books, posters, friezes and CDs to accompany singing the rhymes from memory.

Nursery rhyme books

Nursery rhyme books are useful for reminding you of the nursery rhymes you may have forgotten – as well as introducing new rhymes. For a list of suggestions, see the book list.

Nursery rhyme books also have pictures for you and your child to look at. This helps the child to make sense of the rhyme. Traditional rhymes include many old words that are no longer in everyday use and it can be useful to have a picture showing what a 'tuffet', or a 'fiddle' or a 'pail of water' looks like.

As already mentioned, some children's writers take a nursery rhyme as a basis and build a new story around the rhyme. Older children love seeing familiar nursery rhyme characters in new settings and it shows them that they too can create their own stories around a favourite character. See the book list for some suggestions.

Nursery rhyme posters

Nursery rhyme posters and friezes are fun for decorating your child's bedroom – and seeing the characters on their bedroom wall will encourage them to keep reciting their rhymes.

Nursery rhyme characters also make a good topic for an art project. Get a large piece of card and let your child use paint and collage materials to create their own favourite characters. For a life-sized poster, use a strip of plain wallpaper, ask the child to lie on the paper and draw round them to make the character's body shape.

Nursery rhyme CDs

Nursery rhyme CDs are a useful way of passing the time on a car journey, or soothing a child before bed. CDs often include new rhymes or use slightly different words from the ones you are familiar with. This shows older children that the same basic rhyme can have different versions.

If you have the time and the equipment, you can also make your own nursery rhyme CD – and it's likely to become your child's favourite! Record yourself singing or reciting a selection of rhymes and encourage other family members to join in. Add sound effects such as bells for 'Ride a Cock Horse' or animal noises for 'Baa Baa Black Sheep'.

Other rhyming activities

Apart from nursery rhymes, there are many other ways of exploring rhyming words.

Rhyming I Spy

Play a rhyming version of I Spy. It's easier to pick the item first and then think of a rhyming word. Look around the room and choose an item with a familiar rhyme – such as 'box', which rhymes with 'fox', 'socks' or 'rocks'. Double check that the box is easy to spot and then say;

'I spy with my little eye, something that rhymes with fox.'

Give the child a clue if necessary – 'we keep toys in the thing I can spy.'

Some common objects and rhyming words are;

pen/den	book/cook	table/label	cat/hat	chair/bear
dog/log	plate/mate	ball/wall	bowl/coal	mug/tug	fork/talk
nan/pan	tree/sea	rug/bug	bed/ted	bin/fin	lamp/camp
coat/boat	boot/hoot	dress/mess	scarf/laugh	shoe/goo

'Nursery rhyme CDs often include new rhymes or use slightly different words from the ones you are familiar with. This shows older children that the same basic rhyme can have different versions.'

If you find it hard to think of rhyming words for the objects around you, make up nonsense words – 'I spy with my little eye something that rhymes with smelevision.' Once your child catches on, they will love joining in with their own nonsense rhymes.

Get it right, Mum!

Make a familiar statement, substituting one of the words in the statement for a rhyming word. For example:

- 'We're off to the park; put your cat (hat) on your head.'
- 'Say night night to Nana, it's time for ted (bed).'
- 'Do you want some more feet (meat) with your potato?'
- 'Let's sit down and read a cook (book).'
- 'Let's give the log (dog) his dinner.'

Can your child spot your mistake and correct you?

Odd one out

Draw a series of items with rhyming names, including one item that does not rhyme. Can your child spot the odd one out?

If you're stuck for ideas, try the following;

- rose/toes/nose/cat
- dog/log/frog/cow
- chair/bear/hair/ball
- cat/mat/hat/sun
- coat/boat/goat/apple
- cheese/peas/trees/flower
- bed/head/ted/doll
- ten/hen/men/baby

- pan/man/fan/box

- bee/sea/knee/hand

A white board and marker pen work well for this activity (see the help list for where to buy online). Don't worry if your drawings are a bit wobbly. Young children are not critical – and think of all the great conversations you will have as you help your child to work out what you have drawn!

If you do use a white board and marker pen, you can get your child to put coloured ticks by the rhyming pictures and erase the odd one out.

Rhyming names

Go through the alphabet with your child's name and find the words that rhyme, for example;

- Neil/deal/feel/heel/meal/peel/real/seal/squeal/steel/wheel

- Joe/doe/foe/go/hoe/low/mow/no/row/sew/toe/yo

- Hannah/Anna/banner/manner/Nana/spanner

If your child has a shortened name (Ben rather than Benjamin, Dan rather than Daniel) it's easier to find rhymes. If they have a name that doesn't rhyme with any other word, you can still have fun with nonsense rhymes.

Victoria/Hictoria/Lictoria

Jeremy/Beremy/Feremy

Before playing this game, have a quick run through to check for any upsetting rhymes. Hatty may, quite rightly, object to being rhymed with 'fatty' and Jessie may prefer not to be called 'messy'!

'Go through the alphabet and find the words that rhyme with your child's name.'

Name rhymes

If you, or someone you know, has a knack for making up rhymes, work on a jingle around your child's name. As a child, I loved the rhyme my clever granny made up for me and still recite it to myself today . . .

Hilary pillory

Stick stick stillory

Ree-ro rye-ro

Bandy-legged Hilary

Summing Up

- The rhyming words, rhythms and alliteration of nursery rhymes help your child's language and literacy development in many different ways.

- Nursery rhymes make a useful link between home and school.

- Sing and recite traditional rhymes to reflect your own family roots.

- Clap out the rhythms, add sound effects and actions, let your child finish off the rhymes and make up new versions.

- Share nursery rhyme books and CDs with your child and put up nursery rhyme posters and friezes.

- Use games and activities to explore rhyming words.

Chapter Five

Sharing Picture Books

Sharing a picture book is an enjoyable way to spend time with your child. In this chapter, we look at why picture books are so important to your child's learning and development and how you can make the most of a book.

Why are picture books important?

Picture books help your child's language and literacy development in lots of different ways:

- A picture book is a positive and fun way to settle or occupy your child. If you are a new parent and still feeling your way, sharing lots of picture books will help you bond with your child.

- Picture books make a great trigger for conversation – and young children can learn a huge amount from chatting about the pictures and story. Book-based conversation also helps the child discover that books are an endless source of interesting new ideas.

- Books introduce lots of new words to children – and help them develop their language skills.

- Sharing books with children exposes them to printed words. Seeing letters and words in a book is a good preparation for learning to read.

- Written language is different from spoken language – even when it is read aloud. If you share lots of picture books with your child, they will become familiar with the different forms and patterns of written language.

- Picture books help the young child absorb how stories work. Knowing that a story has a beginning, an ending, a main character and so on, helps them to make sense of stories – and create their own stories.

■ Regularly sharing stories with adults helps the child to see books as an everyday part of their life.

Choosing picture books

With so many to choose from, it's easy to find a picture book that taps into your child's interests, or helps them with a difficult life event such as a visit to hospital. There are also lots of places to find picture books and different ways of building up your child's collection, even if you are on a tight budget.

As a starting point, it's useful to consider the definition of a picture book, and how it differs from other types of book.

What is a picture book?

'With so many to choose from, it's easy to find a picture book that taps into your child's interests.'

A picture book is a book with pictures. This seems rather an obvious statement – but the key thing about a picture book is the importance of the pictures. In an illustrated story for older children or adults, the pictures are only an addition. In other words, the story would work just as well without them. In a picture book, the story is told through a combination of words and pictures and the story would not work so well without one or the other. There are also a few wordless picture books, which rely only on the pictures (and the reader) to tell the story.

At the library or bookshop

Encourage your child to make their own choices when you visit the bookshop or library. If your child falls in love with a book that you don't like, try to go with it. Remember that enjoyment of books is every bit as important as the quality of the book. This does not, however, mean that you shouldn't choose books on your child's behalf. If you love a particular book, your enthusiasm will be infectious and the chances are your child will love it too. A good compromise at the library is for you and your child to choose a book each. Talk about your choices together and emphasise that you are sharing the task of choosing.

Different types of picture books – a checklist

There are many different types of picture books:

- Story books with a plot, an ending, a main character and so on.

- Fairy stories and traditional tales.

- Theme books exploring a topic or concept such as colours, the seasons, shapes, pets, vehicles, toys, going shopping etc.

- Alphabet books and number books.

- Nursery rhyme books – either a collection of rhymes or a single rhyme with pictures.

- Poetry collections.

- Rhyming texts, which may be a story told in rhyme or a theme book with rhyming words.

- Flap books where the reader lifts the flap to reveal the picture or word beneath.

- Novelty books, including pop-up books, books that make noises or books with mini flashing lights, textured pictures and scratch 'n' sniff sections.

'If you love a particular book, your enthusiasm will be infectious and the chances are your child will love it too.'

Looking at the cover

The pictures on the front cover, the title of the book and the blurb (writing) on the back cover can tell you a lot about what's inside. Encourage your child to look at the cover to help them decide which books to choose. Help older children to read the blurb and look out for a familiar author or illustrator.

Matching interests

Look out for books that match your child's particular interests. Whether your child has a fascination for dogs, dinosaurs, dance or football, you should be able to find a book on just about any topic. This can be particularly useful for the child who does not show much interest in books.

Matching experiences

Children love to link a real-life experience with a story and the story and pictures will help them to develop their understanding of that experience. Look out for books about going to the park, going to the seaside, going shopping or whatever fits in with your child's everyday experiences.

A good picture book can also help a child with challenging new experiences, such as starting school, a new sibling, going to hospital or even coping with divorce or bereavement (see the book list for suggestions).

Sourcing books on the Internet

Website sellers such as Amazon offer a huge choice of books (see the help list for details). If you want to find a book with a particular theme or topic, do a search for your theme and see what comes up.

Another useful way of choosing a new book is to click on your child's favourites and then check the 'customers who bought this item also bought' section. If a customer liked your child's favourite, there's a good chance that their other choices will appeal. The reader reviews and 'Listmania' section can also give you some ideas.

'Children love to link a real-life experience with a story – and the story and pictures will help them to develop their understanding of that experience.'

Books on a budget – a checklist

- Make good use of your nearest library.
- Look out for libraries selling off old books.
- Check charity shops, car boot sales and jumble sales.
- Let friends and relatives with older children know that you'll happily give a home to any books their child has outgrown.
- Let people know that a book token is a much appreciated gift.
- Check Amazon and other sites for second-hand books.

Making books available

Settling down for a story after lunch or before bed is an essential part of introducing books to your child. However, it's also good to make books constantly available to your child so they get used to having them around.

Books for babies

As soon as your child starts crawling, put a few board books on a low shelf and encourage them to reach for a book whenever they want. Make sure the books are always in the same place so your child knows where to find them. Stick to just two or three choices and change them from time to time to reignite the child's interest.

As the child grows older and better able to make choices, put out a wider selection to choose from.

Special books

Although it's great to make books available all the time, you may have some special books that you want to protect from your child's eager attentions. Make a space on your own shelves for a book that belonged to you as a child, or a delicate pop-up book, or a beautifully illustrated anthology of fairy tales. Show your child where these books are kept and explain that they are just for special occasions. Apart from protecting the book, this will help the child learn that books are precious and choosing a 'special' book will quickly become a treat.

A book in a bag

Get into the habit of taking a book with you wherever you go. A book can be very handy when you want to keep your child quietly occupied; in the doctor's waiting room, for example. Choose a small paperback that will fit easily into your bag. It's also useful to go for something you can dip into (such as a book of rhymes or a theme book) in case you don't have time to get to the end.

'As soon as your child starts crawling, put a few board books on a low shelf and encourage them to reach for a book whenever they want.'

Sharing a picture book

The following tips will help you make the most of sharing a picture book with your child.

Reading aloud

Don't worry if you're not very confident about reading aloud – your child will not make judgements about your performance! As you become less self-conscious, try experimenting with different voices, accents and sound effects. Do, however, keep to your normal voice with babies who are too young to understand that Mummy or Daddy is only pretending. Older children who are particularly sensitive can also become alarmed if Daddy overplays turning into a gorilla – or Mummy is too convincing as a cackling witch!

'Picture books make a great trigger for conversation.'

Joining in

As soon as your child is ready, encourage them to join in with their own sound effects and actions. Can they bark like Spot the Dog, or stand on their head like Elmer the Elephant? This approach is particularly useful for children who find it hard to sit still. If you are reading a book with repeated sounds, words or phrases, encourage them to join in with the repetition.

Talking about books

Picture books can be a great trigger for conversation. Talking about the story and pictures is easy – simply make a point of responding to any of your child's questions or comments. If it feels uncomfortable to interrupt the flow of the story, remind yourself that talking about the story is just as important.

Finishing the story

Talking about a book as you go along can make the story last for a very long time. If you lose the thread of the story, go back a page or two to refresh your memory. If you don't manage to finish the book, simply paraphrase the story until you reach the end. This is important as it reinforces that all stories have an ending and reminds the child that it's worth sticking around to find out what happens!

Following the child's lead

You can also start your own conversation about a story. However, you may find that the conversation lasts longer if you talk about what the child brings up. Even the chattiest of children can clam up if they feel they are being questioned.

Don't expect your child to ask a lot of questions if a book is unfamiliar. They usually need time to get to know a story before they can start exploring it through questions and comments. A child will also ask more questions and make more comments if they know that you will respond positively.

Making the most of the pictures

The pictures in a picture book play an important part in telling the story and engaging a young child's interest. Whenever you share a book with your child, make sure they can see the pictures clearly. Watch as the child studies a picture, and don't turn the page until their gaze has dropped.

Making the most of misunderstandings

Be ready to respond to any questions and comments about the pictures, particularly when a child 'misreads' a picture. These little mistakes offer lots of opportunity for some fascinating conversations which, in turn, help the child learn a little more about how the world works.

Making the most of a misunderstanding

One of the pictures in Nancy's picture book showed a little boy about to throw a brown rugby ball. 'Look,' said Nancy to her mother, 'he's eating a big huge Easter egg!' Nancy's misreading of the picture was perfectly logical given the shape and colour of the ball and her recent experiences with chocolate eggs. She and her mother had a long conversation about whether it was really a chocolate egg and Nancy learned a little more about rugby balls and chocolate eggs as a result.

Introduce a variety of pictures

When helping your child to choose picture books, aim to include different types of illustration. The artwork in many picture books is superb and a great way to introduce your child to the world of visual art. Look out for books with:

- Photographs, particularly for babies.
- Fun cartoons.
- Quirky collage and mixed-media pictures.
- Beautiful painted masterpieces.

Reading old favourites

Reading an old favourite over and over again is very beneficial for your child – even if it becomes somewhat tedious for you. If a child constantly asks for the same book, there is probably some issue in the words or pictures that they need to explore. You may well find that they ask questions about the same parts with each reading – and as long as you respond, their understanding will grow with each reading. If a particular book is driving you mad, try negotiating. The child can have their favourite once a day, or every other day, but they must make a different choice the rest of the time.

Book series

Many popular story book characters have their own series: Angelina Ballerina, Charlie and Lola, and Thomas the Tank Engine, to name but a few. Reading more than one book in a series helps to expand your child's understanding of the character and introduces the idea that a character can have lots of different adventures. If your child has become obsessed with a particular book, reading a new story about the same character will also give you a welcome break.

Absorbing printed words

Whenever your child looks at a book, they absorb the printed letters and words. This process helps to lay the foundations for reading and writing – and all you have to do is make sure they can see the pages as you read. Drop it into the conversation that you are 'reading the story'. If the child wants to turn over the page too quickly, or leans across the page, explain that you 'can't read the words if you can't see them'. This will help get across the message that the printed words on the page are important. For the three-and-a-half to four plus age group, point to the words occasionally and run your finger from left to right as you read.

Getting to know books

For young children, getting to know their way around a book is an important part of developing their literacy skills. This ranges from the baby discovering how to open a book to the school child learning how to use an index.

As a parent or carer, one of the most useful things you can do is to identify the different parts of a book. This doesn't have to be in the form of a lesson. Simply chat about and name the following features and parts of a book, whenever the opportunity arises:

- The cover – front and back, hardback and paperback.
- The title.
- The names of the author and illustrator.
- The pages – are they made of paper, card, board, fabric?

'For young children, getting to know their way around a book is an important part of developing their literacy skills.'

- The print – does the book use a range of different print styles or colours, and can your child spot capital letters (A, B, C) and lower case letters (a, b, c)?

- A double-page spread – where the picture (and sometimes the words) stretch across two pages.

- The title page – the page before the story starts, giving the title and the author.

- Speech bubbles and labels – often found in books with a cartoony style.

- The gutter – the space where the pages join, creating a deep groove.

- The endpapers – the paper that joins the first and last pages to the front and back covers – often beautifully decorated in a picture book.

- The spine – the outer hinge of a book, much easier to spot on a hardback and usually showing the title.

- The blurb – the writing on the back cover that tells you a little bit about the story.

- The publisher (for older children).

- The ISBN number – the unique number that identifies each book (for older children).

Summing Up

▪ Picture books make a great trigger for conversation with your child.

▪ Picture books help your child develop their vocabulary and learn how stories work.

▪ Choose picture books to match your child's interests and life experiences.

▪ If money is tight, check charity shops, car boot sales and websites selling second-hand books.

▪ Try to be patient if your child wants the same book read over and over again – the child may need to make sense of something in the story.

▪ Help your child learn the names for the different parts of a book.

Chapter Six

Exploring Sounds and Letters

Your child has been listening to the sounds of language from birth. As the child grows older, they can also be introduced to the letters that represent those sounds. In this chapter, we look at how you can help your child to explore and play with different sounds and letters.

What are 'sounds' and 'letters'?

Spoken language is made up of many different sounds. Each sound is represented by one or more letters and by learning to identify sounds and link sounds to letters, the child lays the foundations for reading and writing.

For those who want further explanation, we take a closer look at sounds and letters in the 'Phonics' section at the start of chapter 7. However, as the parent or carer of a young child, all you actually need to know is that:

- Your child is naturally sensitive to the sounds of language.

- You can help your child develop their awareness of sounds by sharing nursery rhymes.

- There are lots of simple little games that can help your child explore sounds through play.

Between the ages of two and three, you can also introduce letter toys such as letter tray puzzles. At this age, your child will be able to discriminate between the different letter shapes – and playing with the letters will help to lay foundations for the systematic learning of letters at a later age.

> 'By learning to identify sounds and link sounds to letters, the child lays the foundations for reading and writing.'

In the rest of this chapter, we look at some activities that will help you explore sounds and letters with your child.

Playing 'I Spy'

'I Spy' is a traditional and much-loved game that has been played for generations. It is also one of the single most useful activities for helping your child's awareness of sounds.

I Spy with initial sounds

The 'initial' sound of a word is the first sound – 'b' as in 'bat', 'sh' as in 'shoe' and so on. Traditional I Spy focuses on the initial sound;

'I spy with my little eye, something beginning with . . . '

When playing I Spy with your child, always use the letter sound rather than the letter name. This means saying 'a' (as in the sound that 'apple' begins with) rather than the name of the letter – 'Ay'.

In the early stages, choose items that are familiar to the child and easy to spot. It's also a good idea to choose a letter sound with several possible answers. For instance, 'c' is the initial sound for lots of everyday items, including 'carpet', 'cat', 'cushion', 'cake', 'cooker', 'coat', 'cot', 'curtain' and 'cup'.

Older children enjoy the challenge of getting the right answer when there's more than one choice – whereas little ones may lose interest if they can't find the answer easily. If you want to simplify the game for a young child, put two or three familiar items on the table for the child to choose from, for example, a pen, a mug and an apple.

Give help and prompts if necessary, and when your child has got the answer, repeat the letter sound – 'Yes, apple begins with a'. The more opportunity your child has to hear the different sounds, the better.

Pronouncing sounds

When playing I Spy, it's important to pronounce the separate sounds correctly. This will help your child when they start to read.

The vowel sounds are fairly straightforward to pronounce …

a as in apple   e as in egg   i as in if   o as in orange   u as in umbrella

The consonants require a little more care. Make the sound as 'pure' as possible – and try to avoid falling into the trap of adding an 'uh' sound. For example ..

- Say 'mmm' (as if you were enjoying ice cream) rather than 'muh'.
- Say 'sss' (like a snake) rather than 'suh'.
- Think of the 'l' sound at the end of 'hill' and say 'lll' rather than 'luh'.

If you want more help with correct pronunciation, www.oxfordowl.co.uk has a clear recording of each sound.

I Spy with end sounds

Once your child has played lots of traditional I Spy, try focusing on the end sound of a word – 't' as in 'hat', or 'k' as in 'book'. The game is exactly the same, except that you say:

'I spy with my little eye, something that ends with . . . '

Give lots of help – and if your child doesn't get the hang of it, go back to playing with initial sounds.

I Spy with middle sounds

With older children who are starting to read and write, try focusing on the middle sounds of a word:

'I spy with my little eye, something with a 't' sound in the middle.'

(mitten, bottle, butter)

You can also choose shorter words with just a single middle sound:

'I spy with my little eye, something with an 'ee' sound in the middle.'

(beans, feet, wheel, field)

As with end sounds, give lots of prompts and if your child struggles, simply go back to playing with initial and end sounds.

Sounds, not spellings

Remember that I Spy is about the sounds of a word, not its spelling. You may find yourself choosing something with an initial sound that is different from its spelling – such as 'Charlotte'. In this instance, say, 'I spy with my little eye, something beginning with "sh"' – because 'Charlotte begins with the sound 'sh' even though it is spelt with a 'Ch'. Don't worry that you might be encouraging incorrect spelling. Your child's spelling sense will develop later as they gain more experience with reading and writing.

At the same time, don't get too hung up on the rules of I Spy. If you don't feel confident with end or middle sounds, it really doesn't matter. The most important thing is to play the game at whatever stage you and your child feel comfortable – and have fun!

'Nursery rhymes and tongue-twisters are great for exploring alliteration.'

Two letters

If an 'I Spy' item begins with a sound represented by two letters, give the sound rather than the letter:

- 'I spy something beginning with ch' (chair)
- 'I spy something beginning with sh' (shoes)
- 'I spy something that ends with th' (bath)

Some more sound activities

Apart from I Spy, there are many other games and activities that will help your child to explore the sounds of language.

Alliterative phrases

An alliterative phrase is where some or all of the words begin with the same sound. Nursery rhymes and tongue-twisters are great for exploring alliteration, as so many of them contain alliterative phrases ('Georgie Porgie pudding and pie', 'Peter Piper picked a peck of pickled pepper'). Try making up your own alliterative phrases and sentences, such as: 'Lovely Leela laughs a lot' or 'Happy Harry often hiccups hard.'

As your child becomes ready, encourage them to join in with their own alliterative phrases. Don't worry about the words making sense. Nonsense phrases (such as 'silly Susie sippy cup') are easier to come up with and much more fun!

Sound effects

Choose a single sound and repeat it over and over again to create a sound effect. For example:

- ch-ch-ch-ch (chuffing train).
- r-r-r-r-r-r (roaring lion).
- ee-ee-ee-ee (squeaking mouse).
- m-m-m-m m (a baby crying for mummy).
- sh-sh-sh-sh (mummy hushing a baby.

Work your way through the alphabet with your child. What could a-a-a-a or b-b-b-b be?

Baa baa black sheep

Sing 'Baa baa black sheep' – but instead of singing 'have you any wool?' choose a sound (such as 'c') and substitute the name of an item beginning with that sound:

- 'Baa baa black sheep, have you any cupcakes?'

Take turns with your child to come up with a whole list of items:

- 'Baa baa black sheep, have you any cupcakes, candles, cats, caterpillars?'

Hunt the sound

'Hunt the sound' is great for occupying children who find it hard to sit still. Say a letter sound, such as 's', and send the child off round the house collecting as many items as they can find beginning with 's'. If you want to be really organised, you can plant some extra items in the child's bedroom (soap, sticks, a spoon, safety scissors, a scarf).

A sound treasure chest

Fill a treasure chest or basket with small items or pictures. Make sure the items fit into groups beginning with the same sound, for example:

- hat/horse/hairbrush/hanky
- cow/crayon/cup/carrot
- book/box/bell/bow
- pencil/paintbrush/pear/pig
- mitten/mouse/mug/mask
- flower/fork/fox/feather
- rubber/ribbon/rock/ring
- doll/dog/dummy/duck
- grape/glove/glue/goose
- teddy/tie/tin/toast

Explore the items with your child and sort them into groups.

Exploring letters

When your child is ready, introduce letters with the following fun activities.

Hunt the letter

Play the game in the same way as 'Hunt the sound' – but give your child a letter card to carry with them. To make the game a bit more challenging, give them two or three different letters. When they get back with their collection of items, help them to sort their finds into letter groups.

Letter greetings cards

Cut out a capital letter from card, decorate it with paint, sequins, glitter, flat-backed jewels and buttons and stick it onto folded card to make a personalised birthday card. Use the same technique to help your child make a name plate for their bedroom door.

Sandpit letters

Hide plastic magnetic letters, foam letters and cut-out card letters in the sandpit. Encourage your child to dig up a letter, say its sound and think of a word that begins with that letter. It's also fun to hide some items in the sandpit and ask your child to match each item with its letter, for example, a necklace to match with the letter 'n', a toy car to match with the letter 'c' and a dinosaur to match with the letter 'd'.

If you don't have a sandpit, fill a large box with shredded paper. You can also drop plastic and foam letters into the bath and use a fishing net to catch them.

Letter foods

- Arrange your child's grapes or cheese chunks into different letter shapes on the plate.

- Use writing icing to decorate home-made cupcakes with letters.

- Look out for letter-shaped cutters; use for making letter cookies and cutting bread into letter shapes before toasting.

Bath-time letters

Once your child knows their letters well, try this simple bath-time game. Soap the child's back and then write a letter in the soap. Can they tell which letter you have written? If they don't get it straight away, give them a clue – 'the animal this letter begins with wags its tail.'

Letter toys and games

Give your child lots of letter toys and games to play with. Invest in a set of magnetic plastic letters for the fridge door and foam letters for letter games. Look out also for:

- Letter jigsaw puzzles.
- Letter-shaped sponges for printing.
- Letter stencils.
- Letter stampers for pressing shapes into play dough.
- Letter lotto games.

Letter stampers, magnetic and foam letters and sponge printing letters encourage the child to explore letters through creative play. This is particularly important for younger ones.

See the help list for websites selling letter resources.

'Invest in a set of magnetic plastic letters for the fridge door and foam letters for letter games.'

Exploring the alphabet

When your child is first starting to explore sounds and letters, don't worry about teaching them to recite the alphabet (A, B, C, D and so on). At this early stage, sounds and letters are much more important to the child's literacy development than the order of the alphabet.

This does not, however, mean that it isn't useful to learn the alphabet – once the child is familiar with sounds and letters. Later in life, your child will need to know the alphabetical order so they can use indexes, dictionaries, encyclopaedias and glossaries.

Try sharing the following alphabet activities with your child. Apart from giving you another means of exploring sounds and letters, you may find that your child learns the order of the alphabet without you even noticing.

Alphabet books

Alphabet books show one or more items beginning with each letter in the alphabet. Modern alphabet books usually picture items that match the sound rather than the name of the letter, for example; 'i for igloo' rather than 'i for ice cream'. They also show both the lower case letter (a) and the capital (A).

There are lots of ABC books to choose from. If your child has a favourite story book character, such as Spot the Dog, Maisy Mouse or the Flower Fairies, check on the Amazon website to see whether they have their own alphabet book.

Alphabet friezes

Displaying an alphabet frieze in your child's bedroom is another way of encouraging them to explore letters and sounds. A frieze clearly shows the alphabet set out from A to Z. This makes it a good starting point if you want your child to learn the order of the alphabet.

Make your own alphabet scrap book

Find a scrap book with at least 26 pages. Write a letter (both lower case and capital) on each page and draw and cut out pictures to stick onto the matching letter page. With an alphabet scrap book everything has a place, so a beautiful sticker or a special photo can also go into the book. Once your child is starting to write, encourage them to make labels for some of the pictures.

'Your older child will need to know the order of the alphabet so they can use indexes, dictionaries, encyclopaedias and glossaries.'

Summing Up

- The sounds of language and the letters that represent those sounds make up the building blocks of reading and writing.

- The traditional game of I Spy is a great way to help your child explore sounds.

- With older children, you can play a version of I Spy that focuses on the end sounds and middle sounds in a word.

- Playing alliterative games helps your child explore different sounds.

- As your child becomes familiar with the sounds of language, play lots of games to help them explore letters.

- Alphabet books and friezes are a great way to explore both sounds and letters and help your child learn the order of the alphabet.

Chapter Seven

Becoming a Reader

Reading is pivotal to your child's learning and education. It's not easy to function in the modern world without the ability to read and once your child starts school, much of their early learning will revolve around literacy.

In this chapter, we begin by taking a look at how reading is taught in schools – and the many different skills that are required for reading. We also explore ways of helping your child become a reader and give some tips for hearing your older child read.

Phonics and learning to read

'Phonics' is the key approach used in the teaching of reading – and once your child starts school, it will play a major part in their literacy learning.

> ### Sound and letter games
>
> Playing the sound and letter games in chapter 6 will introduce your child to the rudiments of phonics.

So what is phonics?

'Phonics' is the technical term used to describe the link between the sounds of language and the written symbols that represent those sounds.

'"Phonics" is the technical term used to describe the link between the sounds of language and the written symbols that represent those sounds.'

Each word is made up of single units of sound, known as 'phonemes'. For example, the word 'ship' is made up of three phonemes – 'sh-i-p'; the word 'chapter' is made up of five phonemes – 'ch-a-p-t-er'. The ability to tune into and recognise the phonemes that make up a word is called 'phonemic awareness'.

For the purposes of reading and writing, the phonemes in a word are represented by one or more letters – called 'graphemes'. In the word 'chapter', the phonemes 'a', 'p' and 't' are represented by a single letter, whereas the phonemes ch and er are represented by two letters.

Some phonemes can be represented by more than one grapheme. For example, the 'ee' sound in 'feet' can also be represented by 'ea' as in 'read' or 'ie' as in 'field'. The 'oa' sound in 'goat' can also be represented by 'ow' as in 'slow' or 'oe' as in 'toe'.

There are two main approaches to phonics teaching – synthetic phonics and analytic phonics.

Synthetic phonics

The English language has 44 phonemes. With synthetic phonics, children learn each grapheme and link it to the phoneme it represents. They can then 'synthesise' (blend) the sounds to read the word. For example, in order to read the word 'feet', the child has to identify the phonemes represented by the graphemes 'f-ee-t' and blend them together to read the word.

Analytic phonics

Analytic phonics is also based on the link between phonemes and graphemes – but it has a much greater focus on spelling patterns. For example, a word is broken into its initial sound (called the 'onset') and the remainder of the word (called the 'rime') – 'c-ake', 'n-ight', 'tr-eat'. Once the child knows these patterns, they can read all the words with a similar spelling – 'bake, lake, make'; 'sight, light, fight' and so on.

Which is the best approach?

Recent research demonstrates that synthetic phonics is more effective than analytic phonics and schools are strongly advised to make synthetic phonics the cornerstone of their early literacy teaching. Learning all 44 phonemes and their related graphemes gives the child the necessary tools to attempt any word. The research also shows that intensive schooling in synthetic phonics can improve a child's reading skills quite noticeably.

However, the challenge with written English is its irregularity and many words cannot be decoded with synthetic phonics skills. Phonics is only one aspect of learning to read (albeit an important one) and your child's teacher will use a number of other techniques, including the following:

Word recognition

As they progress with their reading development, your child will learn what are known as the 'high-frequency words'. The high-frequency words are so named because they regularly appear in written language, for example: 'the', 'and', 'said', 'it', 'get', 'was', 'she' and 'all'. If the child can recognise these words by sight, it helps their reading fluency. Many of the high-frequency words, such as 'the', 'was' and 'she', cannot be decoded using phonics skills – which means they too have to be learnt by sight. For a website listing the high-frequency words, see the help list.

- Help your child by sharing lots of picture books, and making sure they can see the page as you read. This will give them a head start in absorbing the high-frequency words.

Context

The point of reading is to understand meaning – and the context of what the child is reading helps them to read accurately. Young readers are often able to make sense of a word, even if it is not familiar, because of how it fits into the passage they are reading or the story as a whole. An accompanying picture can also provide a child with useful contextual clues.

'The point of reading is to understand meaning – and the context of what the child is reading helps them to read accurately.'

- Help your child by, once again, sharing lots of picture books. This will help the child's understanding of story context. Through looking at the pictures, alongside hearing the words, your child will also discover how the picture can help them to make sense of the words.

Grammar

At a very simple level, the grammatical structure of a sentence will help the child's reading. For example, in the sentence 'Annie ate her dinner', the child is more likely to read the word 'her' accurately because it fits logically into the grammar of the sentence.

- Help your child by conversing with them from a young age. This will enable them to absorb the patterns of language. Reading stories is also important, as it exposes them to the structure of written language.

Different types of reading

'Children need to discover that reading material comes in many different forms and has many different purposes.'

Becoming a reader requires much more than phonics and word recognition skills, important though they are. Children need to discover that reading material comes in many different forms and has many different purposes. For instance, a fairy tale is not the same as an information book; a written list is very different from a poem; a caption does not have quite the same purpose as a label and so on. As your child's reading skills develop, they will be introduced to different kinds of text, and they will discover that reading can be fun, informative, useful, moving, instructive and, most important of all, hugely enjoyable.

In the rest of this chapter, we look at how you can help your child develop their reading skills and discover that reading is a natural and everyday part of life.

Print all around us

Printed words are all around us. Signs, notices, street names, shop names, packets, bags, boxes, the list is endless. Because it is everywhere, print in the environment is a great way of giving your child lots of spontaneous little reading moments.

Making the most of print in the environment

Whenever you have the opportunity, draw your child's attention to different types of environmental print and help them to discover why signs, notices and labels are so useful. For example, tell them you are reading the street sign so you know which way to go, or the instructions on the box so you know how to play the game, or the sign on the door at the swimming baths so that you go into the right changing room.

All shapes and sizes

Look at different types of print – such as the writing on an information poster in the doctor's waiting room or the writing on their juice carton. Can your child spot any letters and words that they recognise? Are the letters big or small? What colour are they? Print comes in all shapes, sizes, colours and styles – and children cope well with the variety, as long as they are exposed to lots of different print throughout their everyday lives.

A packages poster

Many children start recognising food packages at an early age – particularly the bright colours and lettering on snack wrappers. Make a packages poster by sticking the wrappers and labels from your child's favourite foods on a large sheet of paper. Pin the poster to the wall, as close to your child's eye level as possible. Whenever your child has cereal, or a packet of crisps, or beans from a tin, ask them to find the matching packet on their poster. Ring the changes by occasionally adding new packages and labels.

A 'shopping mall'

When you go shopping with your child, take a moment to look at:

- The names of the shops.
- The signs in the windows – such as 'open', 'sale' or 'everything reduced'.
- The labels inside the shop – such as price labels, 'buy one get one free' and 'changing rooms'.

'Whenever you have the opportunity, draw your child's attention to different types of environmental print – and help them to discover why signs, notices and labels are so useful.'

Read the different signs and talk about their meaning. To make your own shopping mall, cut out lots of shops from coloured card and stick them onto a length of wallpaper to make a frieze. Decide what each shop is going to sell, choose names for the shops, write the names on labels and stick them onto the shop fronts. Draw pictures of items for sale to stick in the shop windows, and add some other signs, such as 'sale starts today'.

Reading games and activities

The following games and activities will encourage your child to practise their developing reading skills:

The 'hop, skip, jump' game

This is a great game for encouraging children to think about the meaning of what they read. It's also useful if your child doesn't like sitting down to read or needs to be a bit more active.

Write an action word on a piece of paper or a white board. Help your child to read the word and then perform the action. Start out with simple words that can easily be sounded out using phonics skills, for example:

- hop run jog skip tap pat

You can also include some high-frequency words:

- see look go play jump

As your child's reading skills progress, include more challenging words and help your child to read the word if necessary:

- sing whisper brush kick stroke wriggle wobble tiptoe

Extend the game by adding adverbs:

- run quickly jump high tap gently shout loudly wriggle slowly

Labelling the house

Write the names of everyday objects on pieces of paper or card. Start off with some easy-to-read words, for example:

- jug cup bib mug mat bed pen box bin

As your child's reading skills progress, introduce more challenging words and help your child to read the words:

- chair television fridge sofa carpet door table cushion

You can also introduce extra words to help the child label their home more accurately:

- The blue mug the biggest plant Ali's bed the dog's bowl the stair carpet

Animal antics

Write the name of an animal on paper or a white board. Ask the child to read the word and then pretend to be that animal. As with the previous games, start out with simple names:

- pig dog cat hen ant bee chick

As the child's reading progresses, try more challenging animal names:

- spider horse giraffe gorilla elephant camel donkey

Help the child read the animal name by drawing a little picture of the animal alongside the word.

Treasure hunt

Encourage your child to read phrases and sentences by creating a treasure hunt. Prepare slips of paper with a series of clues and hide them in sequence. Give the child the first clue to read:

- 'Look in the blue jug.'

Hidden in the blue jug they will find the next clue:

- 'Look under Mum's bed.'

Under Mum's bed they will find the next clue:

- 'Check behind the back door.'

Continue with as many clues as you wish, and hide some treasure to find at the end. This is a good game to play with older as well as younger children – as long as they are willing to help little ones read the clue for themselves.

A word flap book

'It's important to prioritise reading at home. The more practice a child gets, the more their reading skills will improve – and teachers have a limited amount of time to hear each child read individually at school.'

Gather together photos, drawings or pictures of different objects, animals or people. Stick the pictures into a scrap book and tape a flap made from card over the picture. Write the name of the object, animal or person on a label and stick the label onto the flap. Help the child to read the word and then lift the flap to check whether they were right.

You can use whatever topic you like for your flap book: animals, cars, toys, family, friends, everyday items – the choice is yours!

Hearing reading

Once your child reaches Key Stage 1 (Year 1), they will start to bring home a reading book. Some children may also be given a reading book during their Reception year, or bring home a 'free choice' picture book.

Reading practice is central to homework at Key Stage 1, and government guidelines suggest that all primary-aged children should read aloud to their parents or carers for at least ten minutes a day.

In this section, we look at how you can make the most of reading practice and give some tips for hearing your child read.

Prioritise reading

It's important to prioritise reading at home. The more practice a child gets, the more their reading skills will improve and teachers have a limited amount of time to hear each child read individually at school. Ask older siblings and grandparents to help hear reading, particularly if you struggle to fit it in yourself.

Reading line guides

Younger children often find it easier to read if they place a strip of plain card underneath the line of words. This masks the words below and helps them to focus on the line they are meant to be reading.

A quiet space

Pick a quiet space and a time of the day when you and your child can relax together. If a child associates reading with special one-to-one time with Mum or Dad, it can help to make reading practice a positive experience.

When to read?

It often works better to have a routine for reading practice. Find a time that suits you and your child. For some children, reading as soon as you get home from school works well. Others need a rest and a snack before starting. Try to avoid leaving it until bedtime, or squeezing it in before setting off for school.

Talk about the book

Look at the cover of the book and read the title. Talk about the story, the characters and the pictures. If the child is halfway through a book, recap on what happened previously and talk about what might happen next.

With older children, talk about different words and phrases. Try picking a word from a sentence and discussing what alternative words could be used instead. For example, in the sentence 'the dog is running fast', what other words could be used instead of 'running' or 'fast'?

Reading for information and enjoyment is the whole purpose of literacy; aim to do everything you can to spark your child's interest in the book and help them to understand what they are reading.

Tackling unfamiliar words

If your child can't read a word, encourage them to look at the picture, as it may hold a clue. Help them to use their phonics skills by asking what sound the first letter makes and so on. Don't let them struggle for too long; tell them the word so that they can maintain the flow of what they are reading. If your child is struggling with lots of words, it can be demoralising. Speak to the teacher about whether the book is too hard for them and ask for advice on how to help your child tackle unfamiliar words.

'Choose books that your child enjoys and read to them often. This will help them discover that reading is fun.'

Encouraging the reluctant reader – a checklist

If your child is reluctant to read, try the following:

- Choose books that your child enjoys and read to them often. This will help them discover that reading is fun.

- Try different types of book; some children are more interested in information books than stories.

- Be patient if your child finds it hard to sit still when you read to them.

- If your child struggles to read for the recommended ten minutes, try splitting reading sessions into two or three shorter time slots.

- Take it in turns to read a sentence or chunk of text. If you want to try this with the school reading book, let the teacher know.

- Discuss your child's reluctance to read with the teacher. If they are struggling, what extra support can be given?

Read anything and everything

Encourage your child to read other things, apart from their school reading book. Read print when you are out and about (see 'Print all around us' on page 76) and play some of the reading games outlined in this chapter. Let your child choose their own books to read to you, including comics and information books. Don't worry if they can read a much-loved favourite fluently because they know it off by heart. Any positive experience of reading is valuable.

Be positive

Give your child as much encouragement as you can, and be positive about their reading skills. Keep telling them how well they are doing with their reading and talk about how many words they can read now, compared with when they started school. Help them to understand that every time they read something, it will enable them to get a little bit better at reading.

Summing Up

- Once they start school, your child will learn to read using phonics, word recognition, context and grammatical awareness.

- Print is all around us; encouraging your child to read signs, notices, labels and other environmental print gives them lots of one-off reading opportunities.

- Help your child's reading development by playing lots of reading games.

- Once your child brings home a reading book from school, aim to hear them read for at least ten minutes every day.

- Reluctant readers often cope better if the ten-minute reading time is broken into two or three shorter slots.

- Encourage your child to choose other books to read to you, apart from their school reading book.

Chapter Eight

Becoming a Writer

Writing enables us to communicate our thoughts, feelings and ideas beyond the 'here and now' of speech. It also means that we can record our messages for posterity, something that humankind has been doing for centuries.

In this chapter, we look at the link between reading and writing, what writing involves and how you can help your child develop their writing skills.

What does writing involve?

Writing is a complex process that brings together lots of different skills and capabilities.

Handwriting

Being able to hold the pencil, form the letters and make your handwriting clear and legible so that other people can read it.

> For tips and advice on how to help your child with their handwriting, see chapter 9.

Putting words into writing

Knowing which graphemes (letters) represent the different sounds of language so that you can set down the words correctly. Knowing the spelling for irregular words that do not follow a set pattern (such as 'their').

'Writing is a complex process that brings together lots of different skills and capabilities.'

Content

Deciding what to put in a story, or a poem, or a list, or a set of instructions, or a caption. Being able to choose the right style of language to suit the content of the writing; for example, poetic language for a poem or clear, functional language for a set of instructions.

Presentation

Knowing how to write from left to right and top to bottom (in English). Being able to write in sentences, with a capital letter at the start and a full stop at the end. For older children, knowing how to write in paragraphs and use commas and speech marks. Knowing how to set out a letter, or a list or a poem.

'Most of what a teacher or parent does to support reading skills will also help a child's writing skills.'

The link between reading and writing

As the previous list shows, writing demands a wide set of skills. Fortunately, most of what a teacher or parent does to support reading skills will also help a child's writing skills. For example:

- Playing with letter toys and games enables the child to recognise letters for reading – and become familiar with the shape of the letters in preparation for writing.

- Learning the phonemes and graphemes that make up the English language. In order to read, the child looks at the graphemes in a word, identifies the phonemes (sounds) they represent and blends the sounds to read the word. In order to write, the child identifies the phonemes in a word, identifies the graphemes that represent those phonemes and writes them down to make the word.

- Picture books and environmental print such as signs and notices give children the chance to look at and absorb written words. This is useful when they start writing for themselves.

■ The patterns of written language are different from the patterns of spoken language. Sharing picture books enables the child to become familiar with written language. Not only does this help them make sense of what they read, it also gives them inspiration for their own writing.

Helping your child to write

Although the majority of activities in this book will support both reading and writing, there are some activities that are particularly helpful to your child's writing development.

'Scribing'

The purpose of writing is to communicate your thoughts and ideas to others, and record them so they can be read in the future. Even very young children can engage in this aspect of writing – as long as they have someone who is willing to be their 'scribe'.

Encourage your child to dictate stories, notes, messages, lists and captions, and write down their words. If you use a white board and marker pen, you can help older children to edit the writing. Read back what has been written and ask them if they want to make any additions or changes. The writing can then be copied onto paper to create a more permanent record.

Scribing for your child will help them to discover the purpose of writing. The technique also helps children to see themselves as writers, even though they do not yet have the necessary skills to write for themselves.

Whenever you scribe for your child, make sure they can see you as you write. This will help them to absorb the process of writing. Make a point of reading back what you have written, to help the child understand the link between reading and writing.

'The purpose of writing is to communicate your thoughts and ideas to others, and record them so they can be read in the future.'

Recognising and writing names

Bags, books, lunchboxes, uniforms and pegs all have name labels – and it's useful if your child can recognise and write their name by the time they start school. Try the following to help your child become familiar with their name in writing:

- Gather together some personalised items showing your child's name – such as stickers, notepads, badges, bookplates ('this book belongs to . . . '), headbands, T-shirts, necklaces, mugs and bookmarks.

- Name plates for your child's bedroom door – either home-made or bought.

- Name labels stuck onto your child's belongings (books, pencil cases, hairbrushes, wellies). The more often your child sees their name, the more quickly they will become familiar with it.

'Writing names on a drawing or painting is a good habit to get into for school – and your child can also write their own name labels to stick onto their belongings.'

Named items and your child's safety

Just one word of warning. When you are out and about, be aware that your child's safety could be at risk if their name is too obviously displayed on a T-shirt, headband, necklace or badge.

As soon as your child is ready, encourage them to write their name. When they are very little, let them make marks and kisses (xxx) in a greetings card or at the end of a letter. As they grow older, show them how to spell out their name using foam or magnetic letters. Write their name with a pale-coloured felt pen and let them trace over the letters with their pencil. You can also write out the name for them to copy. Always use a capital letter at the start of the name.

Encourage your child to write their name as often as possible. Writing names on a drawing or painting is a good habit to get into for school, and they can also write their own name labels to stick onto their belongings.

Not ready for writing names?

If your child has not learnt to write their name before they start school, don't worry about it. Your child's reception teacher will not expect all children to be able to write their name – and pushing a child before they are ready can be very de-motivating. Focus instead on helping your child to recognise their name, or the first couple of letters in their name.

Writing words with cut-out letters

Provide your child with a set of magnetic or cut-out foam letters as a starting point for writing words. Let them play freely with the letters and identify the different sounds they make.

If you notice that your child is beginning to arrange the letters into words, you can help them to sound out a word and find the letters that represent the sounds . . .

- What sound does 'cat' begin with? Can you find the letter 'c'?
- What's the next sound in 'cat'? Can you find the letter 'a'?
- What sound does 'cat' end with? Can you find the letter 't'?

Writing words on a blackboard

A blackboard and chalk is a great resource for writing and you will often see letters and words appear spontaneously as the child explores with the chalk. Standing at an upright blackboard is a comfortable position for the child to draw and write – and the large scale of a blackboard and chalk can be easier for younger children to manage than pencil and paper.

Don't worry if your child comes up with odd spellings. At this stage, the child is relying largely on their phonics knowledge to write, and spelling will usually sort itself out as they become more familiar with written language. For more on helping your older child's spelling, see chapter 10.

Writing words on the computer

Stick labels with lower case letters on your computer keyboard and let your child write 'on screen'. Show them how to use different fonts, sizes and colours.

A computer is particularly useful if your child is struggling to form letters with a pencil. Although it's important for them to keep practising their handwriting, the computer will enable them to record their thoughts in writing – without also having to manage a pencil.

For some tips on helping your child with their handwriting, see chapter 9.

Blank forms

'Be a role model; whenever possible, let your child see you write shopping lists, letters, notes, recipes and so on.'

Young children love filling in blank forms – just like Mum and Dad. The spaces for writing are clearly set out and the activity helps children to see themselves as writers. Make a collection of blank forms by checking through junk mail and putting any unwanted forms in your child's stationery box.

Be a role model

Whenever possible, let your child see you write shopping lists, letters, notes, recipes and so on. Talk to them about what you are writing – 'I'm writing a shopping list so I can remember what to buy at the shops.' If you have time, let them add their own marks to the list or put kisses at the end of a letter.

Display writing

Most parents proudly display their children's drawings, paintings and collages. Show your child that you also value their writing by displaying it alongside their artwork – even if the child is still at the 'scribbling' stage.

Making books

Making your own book is simple and a great way of helping your child to explore books and writing.

Zigzag books

Fold a strip of paper back and forth so that each fold makes one page. Your child can then draw and write directly onto each page, or they can work on pieces of paper and stick them onto the pages.

Ribbon books

Punch a hole in the top left hand corner of some sheets of paper and tie them together with ribbon. If the paper is thin, stick reinforcement ring stickers around the holes. Make a front and back cover with card.

Sewn books

Fold some sheets of paper in half and sew along the fold with strong button thread and a darning needle. If you want to sew more than a few pages, pierce or punch small holes in the pages before sewing.

Photo albums

Buy a mini photo album with plastic pockets. Slip a photo or picture into one pocket and a piece of writing into the adjacent pocket. Mini photo albums are great for making personalised books about an event in your child's life – such as a trip to the zoo, a holiday or a birthday party. The photo album can be reused over and over again.

Ring folders

Buy a ring folder and some plastic pockets. Slip pages of writing and pictures into the plastic pockets. Ring folders are very sturdy, making them a good choice for writing and pictures that you want to store long term.

Ready-made books

If you don't want to make your own book, children's scrap books are cheap and readily available from stationers and toy shops. You can also buy more expensive notebooks with beautiful covers, a good choice if you don't mind spending a bit more on a book for a special project or story.

What kind of book?

Your child probably has their own ideas about what to put in their book – but if they need a bit of inspiration, suggest one of the following:

- A story book.
- An anthology of poems, nursery rhymes or songs.
- A book of paintings, drawings, collages and prints – encourage your older child to write by suggesting that they add captions and labels to the pictures.
- A nature journal – make a record of the wildlife you spot in your garden or park and add photos, drawings and written observations.
- A pressed flower and leaf collection – add name labels for each flower or leaf.
- A photo album – add captions.
- A holiday journal; include photos, postcards, tickets and other mementoes, each with a label or caption.
- A scrapbook about a favourite topic, such as football, horses or pets.
- A general scrapbook of favourite things.
- A recipe book.
- An ABC book.
- A number book.
- A magazine, comic or newspaper.

Different card and paper

You can keep your book simple with ordinary paper and card covers cut from cereal packets – or you can experiment with lots of interesting papers. Try sturdy hand-made paper for the pages and make the covers from card with a metallic, glitter or pearlescent finish.

Decorating the pages

Use paper punches to punch out shapes and stick them round the edge of the pages. Make patterned borders with felt pens, crayons and paint. Encourage your child to think of a title for their book and decorate the cover. Remind them to add their name to the cover as the book's author and illustrator.

Numbers, chapters and contents

Suggest to older children that they number the pages and add a contents page. If the book is long enough, they can also divide it into chapters.

A stationery box

Providing your child with their own special stationery box will encourage them to write. Gather together as many different resources as your budget will allow. Do, however, resist the temptation to put everything into the box at once. Even older children will become overwhelmed if they have too many choices – and adding a new resource from time to time will reignite their interest in the box.

Choose from the following:

- A clipboard and pencil attached with string – useful for writing 'on the move'.

- A small white board and marker pen (supervise younger children when using marker pens).

- Regular and chunky pencils in a range of grades (H, HB, B, 2B).

- Coloured pencils – including metallic, fluorescent and rainbow striped pencils.

'Providing your child with their own special stationery box will encourage them to write.'

- Thin and chunky felt pens (make sure they are non-toxic).

- Ballpoint pens and gel pens in a range of colours.

- Different coloured chalks (for using with a blackboard), wax crayons, charcoal and pastels (for older children).

- Different types of paper – lined, unlined, coloured, airmail paper, scrap paper, blank notebooks and zigzag books.

- Different shapes of paper, such as long thin strips for writing lists and making zigzag books, paper cut into speech bubble shapes, small squares for memos, large sheets for lots of writing and big pictures, and folded paper to make greetings cards.

- Envelopes, in various different sizes (these can be new or used) and used stamps.

- Post-it notes, sticky labels in different sizes, sticky tape and glue sticks.

- Safety scissors (left-handed if necessary), rubbers and rulers.

- Paper clips, staplers (for older children and only when supervised), hole punches and shaped paper punches.

- Stampers and printing sets.

Summing Up

▓ Writing is a complex process that brings together many different skills, including:

> Forming letters with a pencil or pen.
>
> Using phonics knowledge to build words.
>
> Knowing the spellings for irregular words such as 'their'.
>
> Knowing what to write (the content).
>
> Knowing what style of language to use, to suit the content.
>
> Knowing how to set out the writing (the presentation).

▓ Be a 'scribe' for your child – and let them watch while you write as this will help them learn about the process and purpose of writing.

▓ Provide your child with foam or magnetic letters so they can practise building words.

▓ A blackboard and chalk is a good starting point for writing letters and words.

▓ Making books gives your child lots of opportunity to write.

▓ A well-stocked stationery box encourages your child to explore writing.

Chapter Nine

Helping with Handwriting

As we saw in the previous chapter, writing is a complex process that brings together many different skills. In this chapter, we look specifically at the physical element of writing – handwriting.

The beginnings of handwriting

From the moment they first pick up a pencil or crayon, your child is developing the skills they need for handwriting.

Mark-making

The term 'mark-making' is used to describe the young child's free exploration with a mark-making tool – and the marks they create before they are old enough to come up with recognisable drawings or letters

As soon as your child is able to hold a pencil, give them free access to pencils and paper. This will help them to discover that they can make marks – one of the first steps towards writing. Encourage your child to make marks in paste, damp sand, play dough and clay, as well as on paper.

Scribbling?

Although 'scribbling' is generally regarded as a negative term, scribbling as an activity is a very positive stage in your child's writing development. Let your child scribble as much as they want and don't worry about pushing them into drawing something meaningful or writing letters before they are ready. Gradually, the random scribbles will become more controlled and the marks will start to resemble writing, before developing into recognisable letters and words.

'Let your child scribble as much as they want – and don't worry about pushing them into drawing something meaningful or writing letters before they are ready.'

Celebrate mark-making

Greet each new piece of mark-making with a positive response. Write your child's name on every sheet and choose some pieces to display on the wall. If your child goes through a prolific stage of mark-making, save scrap paper and let them make their marks on the back. Introduce variety by giving the child a selection of coloured crayons and coloured paper. You can also turn mark-making into a special greetings card by letting the child work on circles of coloured paper and mounting them onto folded card.

Exploring stationery and mark-making tools

With very young children, stick to chunky pencils, stubby wax crayons and paintbrushes. A chunky pencil can also be used for making marks in sand, playdough and clay. As the child grows older, encourage them to explore a wider range of mark-making tools and stationery (see page 93 for a list of suggestions). You can also introduce smaller tools for making marks in play dough and clay, such as matchsticks and plastic glue spatulas.

Art activities and writing patterns

A number of art activities help early writing development:

▓ Painting enables children to make writing-like movements with their arms and hands.

▓ Colouring in shapes helps to develop pencil control. Encourage your child to colour up to the line and show them how to use small up-and-down strokes with the pencil.

▓ As your child develops pencil control, show them how to draw:
Circles.
Loops.
Vertical, horizontal and slanted lines.
Zigzags.

All of these patterns are used in letter formation; for example, we use a circular shape to write the letter d and a zigzag to write v or w. Older children can make a decorative piece of artwork by creating rows of patterns in different colours.

Holding the pencil

Learning to hold a pencil is an important part of handwriting.

The correct pencil hold

Very young children tend to hold the pencil like a dagger. The correct technique is to hold the pencil between the thumb and the index finger so that it rests on the middle finger. It can be hard to change a child's pencil hold once it is established, so it's worth encouraging the correct technique from early on. However, if your child is resistant to changing the way they hold a pencil, don't push it. At this early stage, the most important thing is for your child to enjoy mark-making.

Be a role model

One way of encouraging your child to hold the pencil correctly is to let them see you writing and drawing as often as possible. Babies and young children have a huge capacity to absorb information. They also tend to imitate the movements they absorb – so if your child regularly sees you holding a pen or pencil in a particular way, they are more likely to follow suit with their own pencil hold.

Pencil grips

If older children have problems with holding a pencil correctly, pencil grips can help. A pencil grip slides over the barrel of the pencil and its shape encourages the child to hold the pencil correctly.

If your older child's writing is being hampered by their pencil-holding technique, it's worth trying a pencil grip. However, you do need to keep an eye on the child's writing as a pencil grip can sometimes make things worse. If the grip forms too much of a barrier between the fingers and the pencil, it adversely affects the child's pencil control. Grips made of sponge often work better than rigid grips because they allow the child to feel the pencil beneath the sponge.

'If your older child's writing is being hampered by how they hold their pencil, it's worth trying a pencil grip.'

Different problems also require different shaped grips. Talk to your child's teacher about trying a pencil grip and be prepared to experiment. See the help list if you want to purchase a pencil grip online.

Strengthening the hand

Holding and manipulating the pencil requires strength in the hand and the three writing digits (the thumb and index and middle fingers). Incorporate the following activities into your child's play to help them develop strength in their hand and fingers:

- Tray puzzles – encourage your child to hold the puzzle knobs with the three writing digits.
- Joining bricks – playing with joining bricks, such as Duplo or LEGO, involves gripping the bricks with the fingers.
- Threading cotton reels or beads – encourage your child to use the three writing digits for cotton reels and the thumb and index finger for beads.
- Wooden bricks – playing with wooden building bricks involves holding and positioning the bricks with the fingers.
- Modelling – squeezing and moulding play dough and clay helps to strengthen the whole hand.

Writing letters

If you want to help your child with writing letters (and your child is interested) there are several activities you can try. Check with your child's teacher to make sure you use the same letter style.

Textured letters

Tracing the shape of textured letters with the index and middle fingers helps your child to learn the letter shape – but without the pressure of writing it on paper. Using textured letters will involve some investment of either money or time on your part. You can buy a set of letters, but they are quite expensive (see the help list for details of where to buy online). Alternatively, you can make your own (see the box below for instructions).

To encourage your child to feel the letters, use them to play games:

- Put a letter in a bag, ask your child to feel it and decide which letter it is. Take the letter out of the bag to check and encourage them to feel its shape. If necessary, give the child clues such as, 'Your name starts with this letter.'

- Use textured letters to play 'I Spy'. Instead of saying a sound, pick a letter and encourage the child to feel its shape before looking for the corresponding item.

- Make wax rubbings of the textured letters and use them to create alphabet books and friezes. Decorate the rubbings with sequins, glitter and buttons.

- 'Write' a letter on the child's hand with your finger. Challenge them to pick out the matching textured letter and then feel its shape.

Making textured letters

To make your own set of textured letters, you will need:

- A set of lower case letter templates (use the same style letter as your child's school).

- Textured material such as sandpaper or felt.

- 26 cards.

- A thin felt pen.

- Sharp scissors.

- PVA craft glue.

To make the letters, draw round the templates onto the textured material. Cut out the letters and stick each one to a card. See the help list for information about downloading free templates.

Air writing

Before writing letters on paper, get your child to 'write' the letter in the air, using big arm movements. Take it in turns to watch each other carefully and guess which letter is being written.

What to use for writing letters

When your child is starting out, give them plain paper to write on. Concentrating on the letter shapes is enough for the child, without also expecting them to get the letter on the line. A pencil is the easiest tool to handle; ball point pens can be too slippery while felt pens tend to splay if the child presses too hard. However, the most important thing is your child's enthusiasm for writing letters. If they insist on using a glittery gel pen with dangly feathers, let them go right ahead!

'Before writing letters on paper, get your child to 'write' the letter in the air, using big arm movements.'

'Felt pen' and 'dotty' letters

Help your child to write letters by:

- Writing letters in yellow felt pen so the child can write over them with a pencil.
- Writing letters in a dot format and showing your child how to join the dots.
- Writing letters and words for your child to copy.

Letter size

As your child becomes more experienced with writing, their letters should get smaller. If this doesn't happen naturally, encourage them to try making their letters a bit smaller. If necessary, use the 'felt pen' and 'dotty' letter techniques to give them some guidance.

You can also encourage your child to keep their letters in proportion. Letters with a tail sticking up (b d h k l t) and letters with a tail hanging down (g j p q y) should be twice as tall as letters without a tail (a c e i m n o r s u v w x z). Once your child starts writing on lined paper, the main body of the letter should rest on the line with the hanging tail below the line. Writing on squared paper also helps the child practise getting their letters the same size.

If you are not sure whether your child is ready to use lined paper, or start writing smaller letters, speak to their teacher.

Joined-up writing

Schools vary as to when they introduce joined-up writing. Many Reception teachers lay the foundations for joined-up writing by introducing letters with 'joining points' (sometimes called 'pre-cursive' letters). Although starting with joined-up writing can seem rather challenging, there are benefits:

- The child only has to learn one way of writing, instead of beginning with print and then switching to joined-up writing at a later stage.

- With joined-up writing, there is less likelihood of randomly putting a capital letter in the middle of a word.

- When a child uses joined-up writing, they see the word as a whole, rather than a collection of separate letters.

If you want to give your child extra support with joined-up writing at home, talk to their teacher.

Handwriting difficulties

It's not uncommon for children to have difficulties with handwriting – and there is a lot that can be done to help.

Talk to the teacher

As always, talk to the teacher if you think your child is struggling with their handwriting. Ask how they are being supported at school and what you can do to help at home. If you are concerned, bear in mind that some children take a while to develop clear, legible handwriting and some never do! Although legibility is important, untidy handwriting is no longer such a huge disadvantage in this age of computers.

The left-handed child

Some children show a preference for their dominant hand in babyhood, while others keep switching until three or four years of age. Let your child use whichever hand is comfortable, but if their left hand is clearly dominant, encourage them to use that hand for writing. It is more challenging for the left-handed child to write because their hand covers what they have written. Show them how to experiment with angling the paper so they can see what they have written. For more useful tips, see www.lefthandedchildren.org.

Posture

Your child's posture when writing can cause problems. If they slump over the table or lean too far to one side this can affect their ability to control the pencil. Try to ensure that your child's chair and table are the right height for them. They should be able to place their feet flat on the floor and have the table at elbow level. A wedge-shaped cushion will put them in the correct position for writing – and a footstool or telephone directory placed under their feet can help if the chair is too big.

Writing slopes

Writing flat at the table can be challenging for younger children. If this is the case for your child, try an angled writing surface. A custom-made writing slope is ideal (see the help list for buying a writing slope online) but you can also improvise with a lever-arched file.

'Some children show a preference for their dominant hand in babyhood, while others keep switching from left to right until three or four years of age.'

Handwriting difficulties – a checklist

If your child struggles with handwriting:

- Talk to their teacher.
- Pay a visit to the optician to rule out visual problems.
- Try a pencil grip.
- Check their posture when writing.
- Check they are not gripping the pencil too hard.
- Check they are not pressing too hard.
- Play games to help them learn their letter shapes.
- Try some exercises to relax the hand.

Writing pressure

Check whether your child is gripping the pencil too hard. If their hands and fingers start to ache, this will put them off writing. Ask them to hold their pencil in the air and try moving it gently back and forth between their thumb and index finger. If the pencil won't move, they are holding it too tightly. Check also for white knuckles and red fingers, another sign that they are gripping too hard.

It they are pressing too hard on the paper, challenge them to make a pattern of lines with their pencil, ranging from light to dark. This will help them judge the difference between a light and a heavy pressure.

Hand and finger exercises can also be useful for relaxing the hand. Try the following:

- Sing 'Rub-a-dub-dub/Three men in a tub' and rub the hands together.
- Wiggle the fingers while you sing 'Incey-wincey spider'.
- Sing 'Twinkle, twinkle, little star' and make twinkly stars by clenching the fists and stretching out the fingers.

Older children will probably prefer to do the exercises without the nursery rhymes!

Letter formation

If your child has difficulty forming letters, ask the optician to check that there are no visual problems. You can also try some of the activities in the 'Writing letters' section to familiarise them with the shapes of the letters.

Letter position

As with letter formation, it's worth visiting the optician if your child has difficulty positioning letters on a line. You can also help by checking the position of the paper. For right-handers, it should be tilted slightly to the left and for left-handers, slightly to the right. Rule over lines with a coloured felt pen so that the child can see them more easily. If they have difficulty starting in the correct place on the left-hand side of the paper, rule a brightly coloured margin and encourage them to write their first letter beside the coloured line.

Summing Up

▨ Once your child is able to hold a pencil, encourage lots of mark-making.

▨ Encourage your child to hold the pencil between their thumb and index finger so that it rests on the middle finger.

▨ Be a role model – do lots of writing and drawing with your child.

▨ Help your child learn the shapes of the letters by:
   Playing games with textured letters and feeling their shapes.
   'Air writing'
   Writing yellow felt pen and 'dotty' letters for the child to write over with a pencil.

▨ Make sure you use the same letter style as your child's school.

▨ If your child has difficulties with their handwriting, talk to their teacher and use the checklist on page 105, to identify obstacles and strategies.

Chapter Ten

Helping With Spelling

As your child's writing skills develop, their ability to spell becomes a more significant part of their literacy. In this chapter, we look at why spelling is important, how to lay the foundations for spelling and suggest some ways of helping your older child with their spelling.

Is spelling important?

Teachers and educationalists have different views about the importance of spelling. Interestingly, studies show that spelling isn't that important to accurate reading. The letters in a word can be completely jumbled up and yet we are still able to read it as long as the first and last letters are correct. For example:

I can raed tihs stencene eevn toguhh the slelpnig is all wnrog!

This is because the experienced reader reads words as a whole. They also use context to help them anticipate the words that are likely to come next in the sentence.

There is no doubt, however, that the spellings in the above example are distracting. Poor spelling can also create a bad impression. Later in life, when your child is taking exams and making job applications, good spelling – or the ability to check spelling and make sure it is accurate – is important.

Laying the foundations for spelling

As we have already emphasised in chapter 8, there's no need to worry about your child's spelling when they first start to write. Writing is a complex process and your child's spelling skills will gradually develop as they gain more experience with written language.

It's also important not to make a big thing about spelling during the early years. Too much of a focus on spelling can get in the way of the child's developing fluency and creativity as a writer – and also prevent them from enjoying their writing. There are, however, some ways of laying the foundations for spelling without focusing on the spelling itself:

- **Picture books**
  Share lots of books with your child and make sure they can see the page as you read. Absorbing how words look will help with future spelling, as well as reading.

- **Sounds and letters**
  Play sound and letter games, share alphabet books and make alphabet friezes with your child (see chapter 6). Getting to know the sounds of language and the letters that represent them contributes towards spelling.

- **Environmental print**
  Take every opportunity to read signs and notices, the print on food packets and so on. Absorbing words in print helps to lay the foundations for spelling.

- **Word books**
  Introduce your child to word books and picture dictionaries – see the book list for some suggestions.

- **Phonics**
  Once your child starts school, they will begin learning phonics and the high frequency words (see chapter 7) – activities that help towards spelling as well as reading and writing. Talk to your child's teacher about how you can support this learning at home.

Learning spellings

Some schools introduce spelling tests as early as Key Stage 1 while others wait until Key Stage 2 (Year 3 onwards). Once your child is given a weekly spelling test, learning their spellings will become a regular part of their homework.

'It's important not to make a big thing about spelling during the early years. Too much of a focus on spelling can prevent the child from enjoying their writing.'

Look/say/cover/write/check

Learning spellings off by heart is only one strategy for developing spelling skills. It is, however, the strategy that parents are most likely to become involved with. The majority of schools use the 'look/say/cover/write/check' approach to learning spellings. This involves:

- Looking at the word for a few seconds.

- Saying the word out loud (this stage is sometimes missed out if a word sounds very different from its spelling – for example 'bough').

- Covering it over with the hand or a sheet of paper.

- Visualising the word.

- Writing the word from memory.

- Checking to make sure that the word has been spelt correctly.

This approach utilises several different aspects of learning, including the 'visual' (looking at the spelling of the word as a whole), the 'kinaesthetic' (learning through movement, in this case, by writing the word) and the 'cognitive' (using the mental processes involved in learning and remembering).

It's a good way of helping your child to memorise their spelling list – and you can also use the technique if the child asks for help with a spelling that you feel they should know.

A list of the Key Stage 1 high-frequency words will tell you which words your child is expected to know by sight (for a website listing the high-frequency words, see the help list).

For some more ways of helping your child to learn spellings by heart, see 'Spelling activities and games' on page 114.

'Use the "look/ say/cover/write/ check" approach to help your child learn their spellings.'

Some more spelling approaches

Apart from the 'look/say/cover/write/check' technique, there are some other approaches you can introduce to help your child tackle spellings.

Separate segments

When your child asks for help with a spelling, get them to break the word into separate segments. This enables them to tackle just one bit at a time.

For example, to spell 'thank you':

- Ask the child what sound 'thank' begins with (th) and get them to write it.
- Ask what comes after the 'th' (an) and get them to write it.
- Ask what sound 'thank' ends with (k) and get them to write it. If necessary, tell them that they need to write a 'kicking k' rather than a 'curly c'.
- Remind them that they know how to spell 'you'.

Breaking the word into manageable bits gives the child confidence, as they discover that they know how to write each bit. In other words, they could spell 'thank you' all along!

Double letters

As we saw in chapter 7, many sounds in English can be written in different ways, for example; 'ee' as in 'feet' can also be written 'ea' as in 'seat, 'ie' as in 'field' or 'e-e' as in 'Pete'. Once your child knows the different ways of writing a sound, you can draw on this to help them with spelling. For example, if they write 'Mikey sat on his seet', ask them to think of some other ways of writing an ee sound. This will help them to come up with the correct spelling – 'seat'.

Common letter clusters

A 'letter cluster' is a group of letters that crops up in a number of words (letter clusters can also be called 'letter strings'). Knowing common letter clusters such as 'ing', 'str' and 'our' will help your child with both their spelling and reading fluency.

Spelling lists often focus on a particular letter cluster; for example, older children may have a list using the 'our' cluster, with words such as 'flour', 'mourn', 'ourselves' and 'journey'.

When helping your child to spell a word, encourage them to spell the letter clusters they are likely to know. For example, a child might ask how to spell 'buying'. Once you have helped them with the first part of the word 'buy', remind them that they know how to spell the second half of the word – 'ing'.

Rhyming families

Help your child to spell by finding a rhyming word with a similar spelling. If your child knows how to spell 'hill', they can also spell 'fill', 'ill', 'still' and so on. If your child asks how to spell 'mill', get them to write down 'hill' (or write it for them) and then ask them which letter they have to change to turn 'hill' into 'mill'.

Words within words

When helping your child with spelling, look out for 'words within words'. For example, if your child is trying to spell 'ladybird', show them how to break it into two separate words – 'lady' and 'bird', both of which your child may be able to spell. Sometimes, a longer word contains one or more familiar words that your child can probably spell, such as:

- listen – *list*-en
- before – *be*-fore
- yesterday – *yes*-ter-*day*
- gloves – g-*love*-s
- about – ab-*out*
- window – *wind*-ow
- often – *of-ten*

If you can build on your child's spelling knowledge to tackle longer words, it will help to give them confidence.

Homophones

'Homophones' are words that sound the same but have different spellings and different meanings – such as 'bear' and 'bare', 'see' and 'sea', 'meet' and 'meat' or 'tale' and 'tail'. If your child writes 'the fish swims in the see', tell them that the word 'see' sounds the same when you say it but has a different meaning. Explain to them that they need to change 'see' to 'sea' and think of a sentence that uses the homophone 'see'.

Learning to check

When your child produces a piece of writing, encourage them to look for any misspelt words themselves. If there are lots of spelling errors, focus on just a few commonly used words. For example, you might want to help a seven-year-old with spellings such as 'about' or 'before', but don't worry if they misspell words such as 'delicious' or 'Leicestershire'.

'When your child produces a piece of writing, encourage them to look for any misspelt words themselves.'

Spelling activities and games

Encourage your child to develop their spelling skills and make spellings fun with the following games and activities.

Ten out of ten?

Type out a short story and include some spelling mistakes that your child is likely to recognise. Let them edit the story on the computer screen, or print it out and give them a red pen. Tell them how many mistakes there are and let them be the teacher. They will love giving you marks out of ten and a comment - 'be more careful with spellings' perhaps?

Silly sentences

Make up a sentence to help your child remember a difficult spelling. The dafter the sentence, the better, for example; 'silly cats have orange oblong legs' (school) or 'Peter Evans often pats Larry Evans' (people).

Singing spellings

With longer words that have to be learnt by heart, try putting the letters to music. Sing them to the tune of a simple nursery rhyme, such as 'Twinkle twinkle little star'.

Spelling hunts

Make letter cards to spell out any tricky words that your child has to learn. Hide them around the house and tell them how many cards they have to look for. Once they have found them all, can they sequence them in the correct order? If you write the letter number on the back (for example, c is number six in the word 'difficult'), they can check whether they have sequenced the letters correctly. This is a good game for an active child who learns best when they are on the go.

Typing spellings

When doing the 'look/say/cover/write/check' method, ring the changes by letting your child type the words on the computer. Show them how to use the spellcheck to check their spellings.

Colourful spellings

If your child likes scented, sparkly, metallic or pearly gel pens, let them write out their spellings using different colours for the letters.

They can also type their spellings using different fonts, sizes and colours on the computer. If they keep forgetting a particular letter in a spelling, typing that letter in a different font and colour may help them to remember it.

Silent letters

Try pronouncing some words as they are spelt to help your older child remember the spelling; for example, 'Wed-nes-day' or 'Feb-ru-ary'. This little trick is also useful for words with silent letters, such as 'knight', 'lamb' or 'white'.

Let your child type their spellings on the computer, using different fonts, sizes and colours.'

Letter resources

Cut-out foam or magnetic letters provide a different approach to learning spellings. Let your child use the letters to spell the words they need to learn. Test them by setting out each word with a spelling mistake – can they spot the mistake and put the letters in the correct order? See the help list for buying letter resources online.

Learning spellings – a checklist

▨ Use the 'look/say/cover/write/check' approach.

▨ If your child struggles with learning spellings or has difficulty concentrating, learn just a few at a time.

▨ Let your child practise their spellings on the computer and use the spellcheck to see whether they have spelt the words correctly.

▨ If your child struggles with a particular spelling, type the tricky letters in a different font and colour.

▨ Make up silly sentences to remember important spellings.

▨ If your child likes stationery, let them use sparkly, metallic and scented gel pens to write out their spellings.

▨ Organise a spelling hunt.

▨ Let your child use cut-out foam letters or magnetic letters to spell the words on their list

---

Spelling rules for older kids

There are a number of rules that can be applied to spelling – although in most instances, these rules are more suitable for children at Key Stage 2. Choose rules to suit your child's age and the level they have reached with their spelling – and keep reminding your child that many of the rules only work most of the time.

▨ Most question words begin with a wh – for example, 'what', 'when', 'why', 'where' and 'who'.

- When you add a silent 'e' to the end of a three letter word such as 'bit', its middle sound changes from a short vowel sound to a long vowel sound:
  - can-cane
  - pet-Pete
  - bit-bite
  - mop-mope
  - cut-cute

- You add an 's' to make a plural (cat-cats) – except for words that end with 's', 'x', 'ch' and 'sh' where you add 'es':
  - bus-buses
  - fox-foxes
  - witch-witches
  - bush-bushes

- Whenever you add 'ing' or 'ed' to a word that ends with a consonant, you double the last letter:
  - sip-sipped
  - rag-ragged
  - bat-batting

- To turn a noun (naming word) that ends with 'y' into a plural, the 'y' is usually replaced with 'ies':
  - fly-flies
  - daddy-daddies
  - bunny-bunnies

- Teach older children the classic 'i before e except after c':
  - achieve
  - receive

You do, however, need to explain that there are exceptions – such as 'height, and 'neighbour'.

- The only English word that ends in 'full' is the word 'full' itself. Every other word ends in 'ful':
  - thankful
  - spoonful
  - fearful

Summing Up

- Good spelling will help your child later in life when they sit exams or apply for jobs.

- Don't worry too much about your child's spelling during the early years. It's more important for them to enjoy writing, without the pressure of focusing on spelling.

- Lay the foundations for spelling by sharing picture books and word books, exploring printed signs and notices and playing with letter and word games.

- Help your child learn spellings by using the 'look/say/cover/write/check' method, typing words on the computer and playing spelling games.

- There are many techniques for helping your older child work out a spelling, including breaking a word into manageable bits and looking for a 'word within a word'.

- Introduce your older child to some spelling rules, such as 'i before e except after c'.

Early Years Guidance

Your child at nursery and school

All Early Years practitioners in England are required to follow the Early Years Foundation Stage (EYFS) guidance for children from birth to five. This includes nursery school and nursery class teachers and assistants, day-care workers, playgroup leaders and assistants and childminders. When your child joins the Reception class at primary school, their teacher will also follow the EYFS.

The EYFS guidance is divided into six areas of learning:

- Personal, Social and Emotional Development.
- Communication, Language and Literacy.
- Problem Solving, Reasoning and Numeracy.
- Knowledge and Understanding of the World.
- Physical Development.
- Creative Development.

Although language and literacy comes into all aspects of learning, specific guidance is given in the 'Communication, Language and Literacy' area of learning. The area of learning is divided into six sections:

- Language for Communication.
- Language for Thinking.
- Linking Sounds and Letters.
- Reading.
- Writing.
- Handwriting.

Each of these sections is divided into age ranges:

- Birth to 11 months.
- 8 to 20 months.
- 16 to 26 months.
- 22 to 36 months.
- 30 to 50 months.
- 40 to 60+ months.
- Early Learning Goals.

Within each section and age range, the guidance lists a number of skills, behaviours and capabilities. These are called 'Development Matters'. Each set of Development Matters leads towards one or more Early Learning Goal (ELG).

The following are just a few examples of Development Matters and ELGs, taken from the 'Reading' section:

- Birth to 11 months.
  'Listen to familiar sounds, words or finger plays'.
- 8 to 20 months.
  'Respond to words and interactive rhymes, such as 'clap hands'.
- 16 to 26 months.
  'Show interest in stories, songs and rhymes'.
- 22 to 36 months.
  'Have some favourite stories, rhymes, songs, poems or jingles'.
- 30 to 50 months.
  'Show interest in illustrations and print in books and print in the environment'.
- 40 to 60+ months.
  'Know that information can be retrieved from books and computers'.
- Early Learning Goals.
  'Know that print carries meaning and, in English, is read from left to right and top to bottom'.

'Show an understanding of the elements of stories, such as main character, sequence of events and openings, and how information can be found in non-fiction texts to answer questions about where, who, why and how'.

The ELGs are statutory. In other words, settings must provide learning and developmental experiences that enable their children to work towards each goal. However, the ELGs are only an expectation of what a child might achieve. By the end of the Reception year, some children will still be working towards some or all of the goals.

Alongside each Development Matter and ELG, the guidance also gives practitioners:

- Pointers for observing children, to assess each child's progress (the 'Look, Listen and Note' section).

- Pointers for helping the child's learning (the 'Effective Practice' section).

- Suggestions for planning appropriate activities and providing suitable resources (the 'Planning and Resourcing' section).

The National Curriculum

Once your child joins Key Stage 1 (Years 1 and 2), their teacher will follow the National Curriculum. The language and literacy section of the National Curriculum is called 'English'. It is designed to build on the Early Learning Goals and continue the child's learning and development.

The section is divided into three areas:

- Speaking and listening.

- Reading.

- Writing.

Speaking and listening

Speaking and listening activities include learning to speak fluently and with confidence, joining in group discussions, listening and responding to others, drama and role play activities

Reading

Reading activities include developing enjoyment of books and reading, word recognition and phonics, reading for information (non-fiction texts, captions and so on) and developing an understanding of story, poetry and drama.

Writing

Writing activities include handwriting and presentation, planning and drafting, composition (the content of the writing), punctuation (full stops, capital letters and so on) and spelling.

Teachers are required to make sure that all three areas are 'integrated'. For example, the teacher will draw on the children's understanding of story (reading) and also use group discussion (speaking and listening) in order to compose a group story (writing).

For more information about the EYFS and the National Curriculum, see the help list.

Changes to the English EYFS and National Curriculum

Following the Tickell review recommending that the EYFS guidance is 'slimmed down', a revised EYFS framework is due to be published in 2012.

The National Curriculum is also in the process of being reviewed, with new programmes of study for English due to be introduced in 2013.

Scotland

The Scottish guidance for Early Years practitioners is called 'Pre-birth to Three: Positive Outcomes for Scotland's Children and Families'. The document gives practitioners information about early child development. It also includes a section on helping very young children lay the foundations for literacy and numeracy development.

The three-plus age group is covered by the 3 to 18 Curriculum for Excellence. The Curriculum for Excellence was introduced in 2010 and aims to give teachers greater freedom than the previous curriculum. Like the curriculum in England, the 'Literacy and English' section is divided into 'Listening and Talking', 'Reading' and 'Writing'.

For more information about the Scottish curriculum, see the help list.

Wales

Guidance for the birth-to-three age group in Wales is called 'Flying Start'. The Flying Start initiative is targeted at the most disadvantaged communities in Wales and recognises that early language development is critical to the child's future social and economic wellbeing.

From the ages of three to seven, children in Wales fall within the 'Foundation Phase'. Practitioner guidance is outlined in a statutory document called 'Framework for Children's Learning for 3 to 7-year-olds in Wales'. As with England and Scotland, the 'Language, Literacy and Communication Skills' section is divided into 'Oracy' (speaking and listening), 'Reading' and 'Writing'.

For more information about the Welsh curriculum, see the help list.

Northern Ireland

The Early Years strategy for Northern Ireland is currently undergoing a revision, with the 'Early Years 0 to 6 Strategy' document still at the draft stage. In Northern Ireland, Years 1 and 2 are known as the 'Foundation Stage'. Along with the rest of the UK, the Northern Ireland Framework for literacy development is divided into 'Talking and Listening', 'Reading' and 'Writing'.

For more information about the Northern Irish curriculum, see the help list.

Help List

Books and nursery rhymes

Amazon

www.amazon.co.uk
Website selling a huge range of new and second-hand books. The 'Listmania' and 'Customers who bought this item also bought' sections are useful for sourcing new books. The site also sells toys, games and stationery.

Books for Keeps

www.booksforkeeps.co.uk
Online children's books magazine with reviews and information about authors and illustrators.

Nursery rhymes

www.nurseryrhymes4u.com
Free website with a large selection of nursery rhymes organised both alphabetically and in themes. The site also has tongue-twisters, lullabies and songs.

Waterstones

www.waterstonesmarketplace.com
High street bookseller's website selling second-hand and out-of-print books.

Curriculum and guidance

Early Years Foundation Stage

www.earlyyearsmatters.co.uk
To download the complete list of Development Matters and Early Learning Goals, click on the EYFS tab.

England – parent information

www.direct.gov.uk/en/Parents
Government site with information for parents about childcare, pre-schools and schools.

National Curriculum - England

http://curriculum.qcda.gov.uk
Information on the National Curriculum.

Northern Ireland Curriculum

www.nicurriculum.org.uk/
Information about the language and literacy curriculum for the Northern Ireland Foundation Stage (Years 1 and 2).

Northern Ireland Pre-school

www.deni.gov.uk
For information about pre-school education in Northern Ireland, click on the 'Pre-school education' tab.

Scotland

www.ltscotland.org.uk
The Learning and Teaching Scotland website. Click on the 'Early Years' tab for information about pre-birth to three and the Curriculum for Excellence.

Wales

www.wales.gov.uk
The Welsh Assembly website. Click on the 'Education and skills' and 'Early Years' tabs for information about the Foundation Phase and a link to the Flying Start initiative.

Interactive online games

Literacy games

www.bbc.co.uk/schools/ks1bitesize
The BBC's website with interactive literacy games for Key Stage 1 children (Years 1 and 2).

Reading games

www.familylearning.org.uk
Website with interactive reading games.

Spelling games

www.kidsspell.com
Website with interactive spelling games.

Language and literacy information

Left-handed children

www.lefthandedchildren.org
Website selling products and guides for left-handed children, including the pre-school age group.

Literacy Trust

www.literacytrust.org.uk
An independent literacy charity with a section for the early years.

National Handwriting Association

www.nha-handwriting.org.uk
A handwriting charity with a section for parents and advice for those with handwriting difficulties.

Read Together

www.readtogether.co.uk
Website for parents about reading with your child. Lots of ideas, activities and book suggestions for different age groups from birth onwards.

High-Frequency Words

www.highfrequencywords.org
Website listing the high-frequency words, along with games and printable resources.

Parenting forums

Mumsnet

www.mumsnet.com
Parenting website with lots of information and discussion threads on language and literacy.

Netmums

www.netmums.com
Parenting forum with lots of discussion threads on language and literacy development.

Resources

Letters and games

www.galt-educational.co.uk
Website selling language and literacy games and resources, including magnetic letters, mini white boards, reading games and listening games.

Letter templates

www.quality-kids-crafts.com
Website with free print style letter templates, lower and upper case.

Pencil grips

www.coolrewards.co.uk
Website selling a range of pencil grips.

Sandpaper letters

www.absorbentminds.co.uk
Website selling a range of Montessori activities – including sandpaper letters in
both print and cursive fonts.

Writing slopes

www.ascoeducational.co.uk
Website selling a variety of literacy resources, including Perspex writing slopes
(search site for 'writing slope').

Special needs

Dyslexia

www.bdadyslexia.org.uk
Website for the British Dyslexia Association. Includes a section for parents and
families, news about events and activities and products for sale.

Hearing

www.ndcs.org.uk
Website for the National Deaf Children's Society. Includes a 'Family Support'
section.

Speech Therapy

www.helpwithtalking.com
Website for the Association of Independent Speech and Language Therapists
in Independent Practice. Includes a practitioner search facility, divided into age
groups from 0 to 4 onwards.

Book List

Picture books

A selection of classic picture books. Some have been in print for years and others are more recent – but all are well worth introducing to your child if you haven't done so already.

Angelina Ballerina
Katharine Holabird and Helen Craig, Puffin
Charming story about Angelina, a cute dancing mouse who is desperate to become a ballerina. For Angelina fans, there are lots more stories, including 'Angelina's Birthday' and 'Angelina and the Royal Wedding'.

Dear Zoo
Rod Campbell, Macmillan
A little boy asks the zoo to send him a pet. But which animal is the right one for him? Simple but perfect – this is the definitive flap book.

Elmer: The Story of a Patchwork Elephant
David McKee, Andersen
Elmer the Elephant is a loveable character and his story contains the important message that it's all right to be different. If your child likes this book, look out for more 'Elmer' stories, including 'Elmer's Friends' and 'Elmer and Wilbur'. You can also buy Elmer as a soft toy, along with other merchandise such as Elmer stationery.

Hairy Maclary from Donaldson's Dairy
Lynley Dodd, Puffin
Lynley Dodd's rhyming texts are second to none. Guaranteed to appeal to the dog lover – and for cat lovers, try the 'Slinky Malinki' series.

Handa's Surprise
Eileen Browne, Walker
Set in Kenya, this beautifully illustrated book has lots to offer, including counting, exotic fruits and African animals. Look out also for 'Handa's Hen'.

I Will Not Ever Never Eat a Tomato (Charlie and Lola)

Lauren Child, Orchard

Lola refuses to eat tomatoes – or any other vegetable, until big brother Charlie finds a way of making vegetables fun. Lauren Child's quirky collage illustrations make this book a bit different – and there are lots of other titles for the 'Charlie and Lola' fan to enjoy.

I Wish I Were a Dog

Lydia Monks, Egmont

Original and clever with warm, vibrant illustrations. Guaranteed to appeal if your child loves dogs and cats.

Little Princess – I Want My Potty

Tony Ross, Harper Collins

A cute and funny tale about potty training. There are lots of 'Little Princess' stories about different events in a child's life – including 'I Want My Dummy', 'I Want My Mum' and 'I Don't Want to Wash My Hands'.

Mr Gumpy's Outing

John Burningham, Red Fox

A wonderful story to read aloud, with a rhythmic, repetitive text and beautiful illustrations. Look out for more of John Burningham's unusual and imaginative books – including 'Come Away From the Water Shirley' and 'Avocado Baby'.

My Alfie Collection

Shirley Hughes, Bodley Head

Delightful everyday stories about a typical little boy. The stories can also be bought separately (published by Red Fox). If your child likes the 'Alfie' stories, look out for the 'Lucy and Tom' series.

Owl Babies

Martin Waddell, Walker

The baby owls are worried when their mother flies off to find food. A delightful and reassuring story about separation anxiety.

Rosie's Walk
Pat Hutchins, Red Fox
First published in 1968, 'Rosie's Walk' is a true classic. Don't be put off by the rather formulaic pictures – there's lots for your child to spot in this simple but cleverly illustrated book. If your child likes 'Rosie's Walk', look out for other Pat Hutchins' books, including 'Titch'.

The Baby's Catalogue
Janet and Allan Ahlberg, Puffin
This is a wordless catalogue of everyday items such as clothes, food and toys. Although it's a delightful book for babies, the witty and detailed pictures make it a great conversational starting point for older children.

The Blue Balloon
Mick Inkpen, Hodder
The blue balloon of the title changes from an ordinary, soggy old balloon into something magical. Mick Inkpen's simple illustrations add to the charm of this clever and unusual book.

The Gruffalo
Julia Donaldson and Axel Scheffler, Macmillan
Delightful rhyming story about overcoming your fears. Look out for other 'Gruffalo' books, including 'The Gruffalo's Child'.

The Tiger Who Came to Tea
Judith Kerr, Harper Collins
First published in 1968, this delightful book has been a favourite ever since. It tells the story of what happens when a tiger knocks on Sophie's door and invites himself in for tea.

The Very Hungry Caterpillar
Eric Carle, Picture Puffin
One of the best-loved picture books ever produced and a must for every child. Check out Eric Carle's other wonderful books, including 'Brown Bear, Brown Bear' and 'The Bad-Tempered Ladybird'.

Topsy and Tim: Learn to Swim
Jean Adamson and Belinda Worsley, Ladybird
Topsy and Tim have been around since the sixties, although the series has been updated for children of today. There is a 'Topsy and Tim' book on just about every life event you can think of, from 'Topsy and Tim: Go on an Aeroplane' to 'Topsy and Tim have Itchy Heads', and 'Topsy and Tim: Go Green'.

You Choose!
Pippa Goodhart and Nick Sharratt, Corgi
A brilliant interactive book of questions, with fun, colourful pictures. If you could go anywhere and do anything, where would you live, what would you eat, who would your friends be and so on. Great for triggering conversation and a useful book to dip into if you only have a few spare minutes.

Nursery rhymes

A selection of nursery rhyme anthologies and picture books featuring nursery rhyme characters.

The Orchard Book of Nursery Rhymes
Zena Sutherland and Faith Jaques, Orchard
A hardback collection of classic rhymes, with traditional-style illustrations by Faith Jaques. A book to treasure.

The Puffin Baby and Toddler Treasury
A collection of classic stories as well as rhymes, songs, poems and lullabies. Different illustrators have been used throughout the book – which makes the collection visually interesting.

This Little Puffin
Elisabeth Matterson, Puffin
'This Little Puffin' has been in print for thirty years. As well as nursery rhymes, it includes finger plays and games with actions.

The Oxford Dictionary of Nursery Rhymes
Peter and Iona Opie, Oxford University Press
This collection includes lots of lesser known rhymes, along with original illustrations and explanatory notes. The introduction is worth reading if you're interested in the history of the nursery rhyme.

The Usborne Book of Nursery Rhymes
This anthology is a good choice if you want illustrations with a slightly more contemporary feel.

Each Peach Pear Plum
Janet and Allan Ahlberg, Puffin
Lots of familiar nursery rhyme and fairy-tale characters appear in this delightful book. The clever rhyming text is easy for children to pick up and recite. For another Ahlberg book featuring nursery rhyme characters, try 'The Jolly Postman'.

Little Bo Peep's Troublesome Sheep
Cressida Cowell, Hodder
Little Bo Peep goes to the library for a book on how to find lost sheep – and bumps into lots of other nursery rhyme characters. Clever, and great fun.

Word books and picture dictionaries
Books to help children of all ages develop their vocabulary.

First Thousand Words in English
Heather Amery and Stephen Cartwright, Usborne
Lots of everyday scenes (at home, at school, at the airport etc.) with pictures of individually labelled items set around the margin of the page. Lots of detail to look at, without being overwhelming. Good for conversation and reading as well as word acquisition. Also comes in Arabic, Chinese, French, German, Hebrew, Italian, Japanese, Latin, Polish, Portugese, Russian and Spanish.

Dorling Kindersley 'My First' Series
Clearly labelled, high quality photographs on a plain white background. Each theme is covered in detail – for example, the 'Body' book includes facial expressions and emotions as well as body parts and clothes. The series also includes 'Colours', 'Opposites', 'Numbers', 'Animals', 'Pets', 'Farm', 'Words' 'ABC' and 'Phonics'.

Oxford Very First Dictionary
Clare Kirtley and Georgie Birkett, Oxford University Press
Commonly used words in alphabetical order, each with a simple definition and picture. There are also sections for 'words we write a lot', 'verbs', 'colours', 'shapes', 'days of the week', 'months of the year', 'numbers' and 'alphabet'.

Reading, writing and spelling

Practical guides for helping your child's reading, writing and spelling skills.

Fun With Phonics: Letters and Sounds Pack (DVD and Book)
CBeebies, BBC Active
The book and DVD take the child through the 44 basic sounds and encourage them to start blending and segmenting sounds in preparation for reading and writing. Aimed at the three to five age group, the pack includes a wall frieze.

Oxford Reading Tree: Read at Home
Oxford University Press
A collection of 12 books, designed for beginners to read at home. The pack includes a guide book for parents with advice, games and activities.

Collins Easy Learning – Writing: Age 3-5
Carol Medcalf, Collins
Activities ranging from pencil control to letter formation.

Best Handwriting for Ages 5 to 6
Andrew Brodie Publications
Letter formation, joining up letters and handwriting practice.

Spelling Today for Ages 5 to 6
Andrew Brodie Publications
Essential words to practise using the 'Look/Say/Cover' technique.

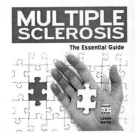